THE WORLD CHAMPION
GREEN BAY
PACKERS
Facts & Trivia™
5th Edition
by
Larry Names

The E. B. Houchin Company

est. 1992
South Bend, Indiana

The E. B. Houchin Company
23700 Marquette Blvd. A-8
South Bend, Indiana 46628

ISBN: 0-938313-30-4

First Edition First Printing: November 1992
    Second Printing: December 1992
Second Edition: October 1993
Third Edition: November 1994
Fourth Edition First Printing: August 1996
    Second Printing: December 1996
    Third Printing: February 1997
Fifth Edition: September 1997

Cover Photo by Jim Biever

Photos from Author's Private Collection

Printed in USA

CONTENTS

PACKER
FACTS

To my two very good Packer friends,

Joe Malecki

&

John Winn

THE PACKER LEGEND

istorians can argue about the birth of the Green Bay Packers until Doomsday, and none of them will be able to claim a qualified date for the inception of the team. Some will say that the Packers can trace their ancestry to the first town team of 1895, that the Pack was born that autumn. Others will say the Packers were born in 1918 because Green Bay didn't have a town team in 1917. Of course, there's the standard belief that the Packers were born in 1919 in the head of one Earl L. "Curly" Lambeau, something akin to Zeus giving birth to Aphrodite in Greek Mythology. And there is the technical argument that the Packers weren't conceived until they joined the NFL in 1921 or that they weren't born until Curly Lambeau was awarded his own franchise in 1922.

The truth of all this is the Green Bay Packers are legendary, and like all legends, their beginnings must be clouded in mystery and intrigue. If they weren't, the Packers would be the Tampa Bay Buccaneers.

Officially, the Green Bay Packers, Inc., claim August 11, 1919 as the birth of the Packers. The Packers' media guide states:

"On the evening of August 11, 1919, a score or more of husky young athletes, called together by Curly Lambeau and George Calhoun, gathered in the dingy editorial room of the old Green Bay *Press-Gazette* building on Cherry Street and organized a football team. They didn't know it, but that was the beginning of the incredible saga of the Green Bay Packers.

"There had been some preliminary talk and planning and that night's decision wasn't announced until two days later, but the big step had been taken. So August 11 is as good a birthday as any."

That much is *almost* fact. *Calhoun* did call for a meeting of all interested "footballers" as he called them, and the date of their meeting was August 11, 1919. In reality, this was an annual event whose history began in 1895 and was interrupted only once, in 1917, because of the World War and the shortage of quality players to form a representative team for Green Bay. The difference in 1919 was the Indian Packing Corporation agreed to sponsor the town team with a donation of $500 for uniforms and equipment.

The Packer media guide goes on to state:

"Actually the initial spark had been struck a few weeks before during a casual street corner conversation between Curly Lambeau and George Calhoun. It was apparently one of those 'Why not get up a football team?' remarks, but once they got interested they wasted no time."

That is the beginning of the Packer legend? What a great tale! "A casual street corner conversation between Curly Lambeau and George Calhoun—" That one is almost as good as Alexander the Great's mother telling King Philip that Zeus was the father of their son.

Mrs. Marguerite Lambeau, Curly Lambeau's first wife, knew the truth. In summation, she related this story:

Lambeau's father, Marcel Lambeau, and she, Curly's sweetheart, wanted Curly to return to Notre Dame that fall, but he didn't want to go. He hated school, and he had a good job with the Indian Packing

Corporation. Even so, if he wanted to play football, he had to go back to Notre Dame. Or so he thought until Calhoun suggested that he could play for the town team. That sealed the deal. Lambeau stayed, and he was elected as the team captain, a title that meant he was in charge of the team on the field.

Off the field was another matter and another chapter in Packer history that is detailed in *The History of the Green Bay Packers: The Lambeau Years, Part I.*

Lambeau solicited and received the financial support for the town team from his employer, the Indian Packing Corporation. The Packers, if you will and as the man wrote in the Packers media guide, were born. They died three years later, but that's getting ahead of the story.

The Green Bay Packers were the class football team of northeast Wisconsin and the Upper Peninsula of Michigan in 1919. They whipped 10 consecutive opponents before being "homered" by another company-sponsored team from Beloit. The 1920 campaign was pretty much the same thing: Packers a lot, opposition very little, with the exceptions of the Beloit eleven and a squad from Chicago known as the Boosters.

Some consider 1921 as the birth of the Packers because that was the year Green Bay joined the fledgling pro league, now renamed the National Football League. Okay, the moguls of the NFL granted a franchise to John and Emmett Clair of the Acme Packing Company, the successor of the Indian Packing Corporation, to field a pro-fessional football team in the city of Green Bay, Wisconsin, for the 1921 season. The team was called the Packers, and it was composed of many of the same players who had played for the Green Bay town team in 1918, 1919, and 1920. The distinction between the 1921 aggregation and its three immediate predecessors? The '21 bunch were all contracted with weekly pay, making them *hired* pros instead of pros taking a share of the collection each Sunday. That's the basis for the argument for 1921 being the birth year of the Packers.

In their first NFL campaign, the Packers were competitive. After four tuneup victories with three athletic clubs and the always tough Beloit eleven, they began their championship pursuit with a win over the Minneapolis Marines, and the people of Green Bay, northeast

Wisconsin, and the Upper Peninsula of Michigan began to believe in their team. A setback the following week failed to dampen their enthusiasm for Curly Lambeau's squad of footballers. They turned out in record numbers for two more home games which the Packers won. The Packers concluded their first NFL season with a pair of games in Chicago against the Cardinals and the Decatur Staleys. They tied the Redbirds, but the Starchmakers from Decatur whipped them soundly, 20-0.

Time for more legend.

The Packers media guide states:

> "… But the team was so successful by 1921 that Lambeau was backed by two officials of the packing plant in obtaining a franchise in the new national pro football league that had been formed in 1920. Cash customers didn't quite pay the freight and at the end of the season it had to be forfeited."

The first sentence of that statement is somewhat true, but not completely. The second statement is pure company-line bunkum.

Some historians subscribe to this tale:

Curly Lambeau used some college players in a non-league contest in Milwaukee against the Racine Legion in early December that was billed as the Wisconsin State Championship game. A Chicago sportswriter found out about it and blew the whistle on the Packers. Incensed by this infraction of the rules, the NFL moguls demanded the forfeiture of the Green Bay franchise, and the Clairs complied.

Now the truth.

Lambeau used college players all right, but it was in Green Bay's game against the Decatur Staleys. George Halas's collegiate ringers spotted Lambeau's collegiate ringers, and Halas told the Chicago newspapers about it. The NFL demanded the forfeiture of the franchise, and the Clairs complied.

Why is the latter story true? Lets go back to 1921 and find out.

Most sportswriters, those in Chicago in particular, were opposed to professional football. Only those in small towns, such as Green Bay, bothered to attend games and write about the local team. When the big city scribes wrote about the pro game, they did so as a way of degrading the pros. The alleged game was held in Milwaukee. Why would a Chicago sportswriter be in the Cream City covering a game that didn't have a Chicago team in it? Why would a Chicago sportswriter care about a game in Milwaukee between two small town teams such as Green Bay and Racine? Why would the NFL care about the Packers using college players in a *non-league* game, especially since the circuit's rules didn't forbid such use of college players? One of the players used by Lambeau was Notre Dame's Heartley "Hunk" Anderson, a former teammate of Lambeau's and a native of the Upper Peninsula of Michigan. George Halas coveted Anderson's services, and if Green Bay was in the league, Anderson would more than likely sign with the Packers to play in '22. Therefore, Green Bay had to be removed from the NFL. Halas blew the whistle to the Chicago press, and the NFL gave in to their pressure to get rid of Green Bay from the loop.

More legend:

Lambeau's friend Don Murphy sold his car to loan Curly the money to buy back the franchise that the Clairs had forfeited.

The truth:

Curly Lambeau so loved football and he wanted so badly to play in the NFL that he went to the league meeting in January of '22 to apply for a new franchise for Green Bay. He didn't get it. Leastways, not at that meeting. For months, the league officials put off a final decision on his request. When they did make a decision, they told Curly that he could have his franchise if he could raise $1,000 as security against folding. Lambeau succeeded in raising the money by forming a corporation whose principal owner was Nathan Abrams.

Some historians have chosen June 24, 1922 as the birthday of the Green Bay Packers because that was the day Lambeau was awarded a franchise in the NFL and that franchise has continued without interruption to the present. They have a sound argument, too.

All that debating aside, the facts are these:

The city of Green Bay, Wisconsin, had a professional football team as early 1895. That team played every fall until 1917 when it died due to the first World War. In 1918, Nathan Abrams and George

Calhoun created a new town team from the ashes of the first one. In 1919, the Indian Packing Corporation supported the town team, which was then nicknamed the Packers and had Curly Lambeau as its captain and leader. John and Emmett Clair were awarded a franchise in the NFL in 1921, and they hired Curly Lambeau to field a team for them. The Clairs forfeited their franchise January 28, 1922, and Lambeau was awarded a new franchise June 24, 1922. The team was born in 1895, went comatose in various years, then was resurrected for good in 1918. The financial support of the team was born in 1919 when the Indian Packing Corporation backed the town boys. It died in 1922 when the Clairs threw in the towel. *Lambeau resurrected the team when he was awarded a franchise June 24, 1922.* Nathan Abrams, Lambeau, Calhoun, et al, and the first corporation started up in 1922 to back the team. A new corporation, the one that has remained in existence with some revisions ever since, was begun in 1923.

Taking all that into consideration, when were the Green Bay Packers born? Like the media guide states, "… August 11 is as good a birthday as any." But the birth of the *current* Green Bay Packers occurred when Earl L. Lambeau was granted a franchise in the NFL on June 24, 1922. That makes Lambeau the founder of the Packers.

So what's the big deal over when the Packers were founded? Bragging rights. The Bears and Packers have argued for years over which team was the oldest in the NFL.

Packer fans shouldn't be disillusioned that Curly Lambeau didn't found the Packers in 1919. They can take consolation in the fact that George Halas didn't found the Chicago Bears in 1920 as his biographer and the NFL would have everybody believe. The truth of that tale is the Staley Starch Company fielded a company football team the year before Halas went to work for the company. Halas was hired to take over that team and the company baseball team, which was also in existence before his employment there.

However, Halas really did start the franchise now known as the Chicago Bears. Halas and partner Ed Sternaman were given a franchise for the city of Chicago January 28, 1922. The franchise held by the Staley company was returned to the NFL at that same meeting. *It was never <u>transferred</u> to Halas because of a dispute between Halas* *and another applicant for the Staley franchise.* That makes Halas and his partner the founders of the current franchise known as the Chicago Bears.

Under those conditions, Lambeau is the founder of the current team known as the Green Bay Packers.

So the Bears are the older of the two franchises, but the Bears are not the oldest team in the NFL. That honor belongs to the Cardinals, now of Phoenix, Arizona, but originally known as the Morgan Athletic Club of Chicago, Illinois, founded in 1898. The Cardinals are an original member of the NFL, possessing a franchise that has been *transferred* from one owner to the next but which has never been returned to the NFL, unlike the Bears and Packers.

Confused? That's what legends are supposed to do, and the Packer legend is a dandy at that, isn't it?

ROBERT BROOKS

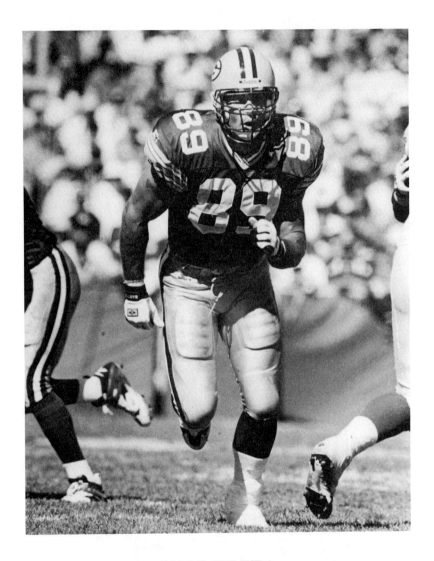

MARK CHMURA

THE
FIRST TRIPLE CHAMPS

T he three consecutive National Football League titles won by the Packers under Vince Lombardi in the 1960s, climaxed by Super Bowls I and II, have often been publicized as the ultimate achievement in football history. Yes, they were remarkable; incredible even, if you will. But the exploits of Bart Starr, Paul Hornung, Jim Taylor, and company weren't the pinnacle of NFL history. That distinction rests in another era.

Officially, the Green Bay Packers won back-to-back-to-back crowns in 1929, 1930, and 1931, and the record of those teams was even more spectacular than those of the Packers of the '60s. Records aside, Green Bay's masterful achievement under Curly Lambeau was all the more amazing considering that it was done in an age when no college draft existed to balance the level of competition, that it was done in an era when most players were often free to jump to any team from year-to-year, and that it was done at a time when the best players forsook professional football after a year or two to take up the more reliable and financially rewarding career of college football coaching; all of these factors making it nearly impossible to develop a football dynasty. But somehow Lambeau did it in little Green Bay.

In 1929, the Packers went undefeated, posting 12 wins, no losses, and one tie; and in the three-year span of 1929-31, they compiled 34 wins against five losses and two ties. This was an outstanding accomplishment, and it didn't come easy for the Packers.

Curly Lambeau had begun recruiting players from beyond the Green Bay area in the early 1920s.

The first player with a reputation that went beyond the borders of Wisconsin to join the Packers was Howard "Cub" Buck who played college ball at the University of Wisconsin and one year of pro ball with the Canton Bulldogs. Buck was a giant of a center who anchored the Packer line from 1921 through 1925.

The next year saw Francis "Jug" Earpe come over from the Rock Island Independents early in the campaign. Earpe spent his collegiate days at little Monmouth College in Iowa. When he joined the Packers, he took over the center spot as Buck moved to tackle.

Besides Earpe, Howard "Whitey" Woodin, a guard from Marquette, signed on with the Packers in 1922. Woodin started the year with the Racine Legion before gaining his release and heading north. He would remain with the Packers for 10 solid seasons, including the three championship years,

In 1924, the Packers acquired the great punter and running back from Nebraska, Verne Lewellen. Carl Lidberg, a fullback from Minnesota, joined the team in 1926, and in 1927, two former Marquette stars, end Lavvie Dilweg and quarterback Red Dunn, put on the Packer colors. Tom Nash, an end from Georgia, signed in 1928, and so did the notorious Johnny Blood.

1928 was also the year that the little town of Green Bay made its first big splurge on the national sports scene when the Packers beat the New York Giants at the Polo Grounds, 7-0. Tim Mara launched the Giants as a new member of the National Football League three years before, but the Packers didn't play the Gothamites that season or the next two. The Giants defeated the Packers, 6-0, in their first encounter earlier in the 1928 season at Green Bay, which made the New Yorkers heavy favorites on their home turf. The New York press made a lot of jokes about the yokels from Wisconsin, but when the Packers withstood every challenge on the field, it made headlines in all the metropolitan newspapers. Once again, David slew Goliath.

The Packers finished the 1928 campaign with a 6-4-3 record that was topped off with a 6-0 win over the Bears in Chicago on the last day of the season. This victory began an incredible string of 22 games without a defeat for Green Bay.

Three all-time Packer greats joined the team in 1929: Cal Hubbard, Mike Michalske, and Bo Molenda. All three came from the defunct New York Yankees, and they were all very happy to settle down in a town like Green Bay. The football Yankees had been founded in 1925 by the big-time sports promoter C.C. "Cash-and-Carry" Pyle as a traveling sideshow act to exhibit the talents of the immortal Red Grange. The Yankees had no home field and played all their games on the road. The year Michalske joined them out of Penn State, they played 36 games in one season. They would often play a game one afternoon, hop on a train, and travel to the next town where they would either play the next day or the day after.

In those days, football players carried all their own gear wherever they went, and their total outfit could be held in one handbag. Very little was provided in the way of dressing quarters. Michalske recalled once that when they played in Pottsville, Pennsylvania, the team dressed in the fire station two blocks away from the stadium, then ran down to the field for the game and dragged their butts back afterwards. When the Packers played the Staten Island Stapletons, they dressed in their hotel rooms in downtown Manhattan, took a bus to the Staten Island ferry landing, then rode the boat over to the island where they proceeded on foot to the stadium. Imagine the excitement that a football team in full uniform, minus their shoes of course, must have created on the Staten Island ferry.

Michalske and Hubbard had played side by side when they were with the Yankees, and very soon they took over anchoring the left side of the Packer line. Dilweg was at left end. With Jug Earpe at center, Woodin and Paul Minnick shared the right guard spot. Claude Perry was at right tackle, and Tom Nash at right end.

The Packers employed the Notre Dame box in the backfield, which Lambeau had learned under Knute Rockne. Quarterback Red Dunn lined up two yards behind the center. Bo Molenda and Carl Lidberg alternated at fullback, flanked right or left just behind the line. Verne Lewellen was at left half, and Johnny Blood was at right. Dunn, the quarterback or spinner as the position was sometimes known in football circles of those days, could hand off to any one of the three backs or drop back to pass.

On defense, the 1929 Packers used a seven-man line with a fullback (linebacker) behind it, the halfbacks covering the outside, and Dunn deep as the safety. Gradually, however, they experimented with a "roving center," and Michalske wound up the next year as a weak side linebacker.

Dunn was an experienced field general who had played with the Milwaukee Badgers and the Chicago Cardinals after graduating from Marquette. He, Lewellen, and Lidberg had already had two seasons together in the Packer backfield and a partial season with Blood when Molenda came along.

Blood was one of the most colorful players ever to wear a Packer uniform. He had a well-deserved reputation as a lady's man, and he also liked alcoholic beverages. Lambeau roomed Blood with Michalske whenever they were on the road, thinking that the older and more staid Michalske would keep Blood in line. However, even "Iron Mike" failed sometimes at that assignment.

The late John Torinus, Sr., who cut his journalistic teeth under the tutelage of the first great Packer promoter and historian George Whitney Calhoun told a great tale about Blood in his history of the Packers, *The Packer Legend.*

I happened to be present one Friday evening in the New Yorker Hotel when the Packers had come to the "Big Apple" to play the Giants on Sunday. Blood had been out beyond the curfew hour and awoke Michalske upon returning to invite him to have a nightcap. Mike allowed as though he would, but he complained that there was no ice. Blood said that was no problem: he could take care of that. He disappeared for about a half hour, then reappeared, marching through the hotel lobby to the elevator carrying a cake of ice, complete with tongs.

The next morning Blood was still in a state of inebriation, and Michalske suggested to him that he probably had the flu and would so inform Lambeau at practice. But Blood was not going to miss practice for a little thing like "bottle" flu.

That morning I was helping tag balls for the kickers who were practicing. Everyone stood around and watched as Blood tried to meet the ball with his foot during his turn. About the second try, he fell flat on his back, and Lambeau came storming over and fired him on the spot. He might have stayed fired, too, if Michalske and others on the team hadn't prevailed on Lambeau that evening to reinstate him. He went on to play a spectacular game against the Giants on Sunday.

Blood was one of the key elements in making the Packer passing game click, for he had the knack of coming down with the ball in a crowd. He left the Packers after the 1936 season and went to the Pittsburgh Steelers where he played three more years before becoming head coach there.

One of the most famous games in Packer history occurred late in that first championship season of 1929 when the Packers again engaged the New York Giants at the Polo Grounds. They beat them, 20-6, and only 11 men played the game on offense and defense for the Packers until the final minute of the play when Lambeau sent Paul Minnick into the game to substitute for Jim Bowdoin. Curly wanted to give the rookie Minnick a little playing time, but Bowdoin was so angry at being replaced that he charged back into the game two plays later and kicked Minnick out.

Hubbard was a giant of a man among players of those days and would rank pretty well with the giant tackles of the present era. He had great upper body strength and could easily handle the opposing tackle and end when playing defense and often took on the whole side of the opposing line when playing offense. He was also a coach on the field, and he, Michalske, Dunn, and Blood frequently made up plays as they went along, much to Curly Lambeau's chagrin and embarrassment.

Red Grange left the Yankees after the 1927 season and joined the Chicago Bears. One of the largest crowds in Packer history up to that time turned out at old City Stadium for the Bear game but were disappointed when Grange could not play because of an ankle sprain he had suffered the previous Sunday. Despite Grange's presence with the Bears, however, the Packers beat their long-time enemy three times during that first championship season by scores of 23-0, 14-0, and 25-0. The third Bear game was played in Chicago, and when the team arrived home that Sunday evening on the Chicago and Northwestern Railroad, hometown fans lined the tracks for the five miles between DePere and Green Bay with kerosene torches. Then the team was paraded from the station to the Beaumont Hotel for a giant victory celebration.

The Packers were each given a watch as a memento of their second championship in 1930, but after the third title in 1931, they were merely told it was nice to have them home. In his later years when being interviewed by John Torinus, Sr., for his history of the Packers, Michalske recalled that Green Bay fans had already grown a little complacent about titles.

The Packers almost made it four crowns in a row in 1932. They played two tough games against the Bears, tying the first, 0-0, and winning the second, 2-0. They were undefeated when they again challenged the Giants in New York and lost, 6-0. They were still leading the league until the last two games when they lost to Portsmouth, 19-0, then were beaten out of the championship by the Bears in Chicago, 9-0. The Packers actually won more games than the Bears did but lost the title by percentage points. The Bears tied six games that season and ties counted as nothing under the system then in use. Chicago's unreal 7-1-6 record amounted to the same as a 7-1 mark, while Green Bay's 10-3-1 was the equivalent of a 10-3 season. In percentages, the Packers were .769 and the Bears came in at .875. Using the modern system of figuring the standings where each tie is figured as half a loss and half a win, the Bears would have had a mark of .714, while the Packers would have finished at .750, giving Green Bay its fourth straight title. Even using the National Hockey League's system where a team receives two points for each win and one point for each tie, the Packers would have tallied 21 points to the Bears' 20, again giving them the title that they had earned on the field.

With all the historical revisionism going on these days, maybe the NFL should correct that little piece of injustice and award the 1932 crown to Green Bay, giving the Packers four consecutive NFL championships. Now that's a feat that no NFL team is ever likely to equal, least of all to surpass.

BRETT FAVRE and RON WOLF

LEROY BUTLER

NO HUTSON,
NO PANACHE

T hroughout the whole world, 1945 was a year of enormous change. In some respects, life returned to normal. In others, it would never be the same again.

For the National Football League, 1945 marked the end of two eras and the beginning of several new ones.

The Cleveland Rams won the Western Division title in 1945, making them the first team other than the Green Bay Packers or the Chicago Bears to wear the crown since 1935 when the Detroit Lions ascended to the top of the division. Furthermore, the Rams won the NFL championship, breaking the stranglehold the "Big Four" had had on it since 1936. During those nine years (1936-44), the Bears and Packers each won three NFL titles; the Washington Redskins two; and the New York Giants one. Also, either the Giants or Redskins won the Eastern Division title in each of those nine years.

1945 was also the year Don Hutson played his last game for the Green Bay Packers. His retirement left such a gaping hole in Green

Bay's offense that it wouldn't be filled by any one man for more than four decades.

When he hung up his cleats for good, Don Hutson was the owner of every Green Bay and nearly every NFL pass receiving and scoring record extent, whether the mark was for one quarter, one game, one season, or a career. In 11 years, he played in 117 of 120 regular season games, four NFL title games, and one divisional playoff game. Two of the contests he missed were the last two tilts of the 1935 season when he was sidelined with appendicitis.

Hutson's most astounding marks for one quarter were those he set against the Lions in Green Bay in 1945 when he caught four TD passes and booted five PATs for a total of 29 points in the second period of that game. Even in a later age when passing became much more dominant in the pro game, no one would catch four touchdown passes or score 29 points in a single quarter.

It must be remembered that Hutson played in an era when passing was an alternative to running, not the other way around. If a team threw over 20 passes in a game, it was usually because their opponent had a lead of eight points or more in the fourth quarter and the need to score quickly was urgent. Although the Packers routinely threw 20-25 passes in games in which they usually held the upper hand, not all of the aerials were aimed in Hutson's direction. Milt Gantenbein, Harry Jacunski, Carl Mulleneaux, and a host of good pass-catching backs were around to take the pressure off Hutson during his career.

Also, it must be noted that, because he was the premier receiver of his time, Hutson was double-teamed or triple-teamed by every defense he went up against after his first year in the league. That made his single-game record of 14 catches against the New York Giants in 1942 all the more remarkable. By the way, the previous mark was 13 catches in one game, and Hutson set that record earlier in 1942 against the Rams.

Oddly, Hutson didn't set a single-game yardage mark against the Giants, but he did set one against the Rams when he caught 13 passes for 209 yards. This broke the mark he had set just 10 days earlier against the Cards when he gained 207 yards on five catches. His best game was against Brooklyn in 1943 when he racked up 237 yards on eight receptions.

His single-season marks were all eventually beaten, but only a few of them were broken within the number of games he played each year. In the years that Hutson played, the seasons were only 12 games long in 1935 and 1936, 11 games from 1937 thru 1942, and 10 games from 1943 thru 1945. His single-season marks included most catches, 74 in 1942; most yards, 1,211 in 1942; and most TDs, 17 in 1942. Broken down to averages, that year Hutson caught 6.73 passes for 110.1 yards and 1.55 TDs per game. Those real season numbers stood as the best ever for decades before being broken, and only one of his per game averages had been topped at the time of this writing. Sterling Sharpe broke it when he caught 108 passes in 16 games in 1992 for an average of 6.75 catches per game; then he broke his own mark the following season when hauled in 112 passes in 16 games for an average of 7.0 receptions per game.

TIME OUT:

Sharpe's records have since been broken by a couple of great receivers, but because neither of them did it with the Packers, they aren't worth mentioning here.

TIME IN:

For his career, Hutson retired with 488 catches for 7,991 yards and 99 touchdowns. Per season, those numbers average out to 44.36 receptions for 726.45 yards and 9 TDs. Per game, he averaged 4.17 catches for 68.30 yards and 0.85 touchdowns. Hutson's averages per season have all been beaten in succeeding years, and some of his per game averages for a career were in jeopardy at the time of this writing.

TIME OUT:

Players whose careers are still in progress aren't considered here. Sharpe's career might be over at this time; then again, it might not be. Until his career is officially over, his averages can't be considered as besting Hutson's. Should his career be resumed, it wouldn't take many games played without catching a pass or only catching a pass or two to drop his averages below Hutson's. For now, Hutson is still the king of all receivers in NFL history.

TIME IN:

Carried one step further by taking the averages of Hutson's best season, 1942, and carrying them out to 16 games in a season, Hutson would have caught 107 passes for 1,761 yards and 24 touchdowns. The records for those three one-season categories as of this writing were 123 receptions by Herman Moore of the Lions in 1995 in 16 games; 1,746 yards by Charley Hennigan, Houston Oilers, 1961, in 14 games; and 22 TDs by Jerry Rice, San Francisco 49ers, 1987, in 15 games. Hennigan's yardage record deserves an asterisk in that he achieved it against inferior competition in the fourth American Football League's second season. He came close to that mark once more in '64, but again he was playing against inferior competition in the AFL.

The most incredible aspect of Hutson's career was his statistics for 1943 thru 1945. Most receivers slow down when they hit 30 years of age, but not Hutson. He continued to pile up numbers. Even so, his stats could have been much greater than they were, considering the quality of competition he faced in those years, but the numbers weren't better because Arnie Herber was gone by then and Cecil Isbell retired after the 1942 campaign. If Isbell had stayed in the game instead of turning to coaching, he and Hutson would have had one field day after another against the war time replacement players of the NFL. Unfortunately, Isbell quit the league, and Hutson was left with passers that he made look good.

When Hutson quit playing, the Packers were virtually left without a passing attack because Lambeau had no receivers that came anywhere near the best of the rest in the NFL. To make matters worse, Green Bay had no passer like a Luckman or a Baugh or even a Cecil Isbell or Arnie Herber to compensate for the lack of pass-catchers.

Put as simply as possible, Don Hutson was to professional football what Babe Ruth was to Major League baseball and Michael Jordan is to the National Basketball Association.

Don Hutson passed away June 26, 1997. While he was still playing, he received one of the greatest tributes of all time from none other than George Halas, old Papa Bear himself. "Hutson is so extraordinary that I concede him two touchdowns a game and just hope we can score more."

Hutson was the first Packer player to have his jersey retired. His #14 was retired during a ceremony at old City Stadium in 1951. He was also an original inductee into the Pro Football Hall of Fame in 1963 and the Packer Hall of Fame.

As a person, no one ever said an unkind word about Don Hutson. He was admired by all who knew him. If anyone ever exemplified what it means to be a Packer on and off the field and in life after football, it was Don Hutson.

GABE WILKINS

THE ALL-TIME
PACKERS OF 1946

Early in the 1946 season the Green Bay *Press-Gazette* started a fan poll to name the "All-Time Packers" team. The results of the voting were announced weekly in the newspaper as if they were conducting a horse race. Various past players and officials of Packerdom were asked to name their "All-Time" team, and their choices were periodically printed in the paper to spur the fans to vote. Less than 2,000 voters cast ballots in spite of all the prodding. The final tally was published in the November 19 issue, but it contained few surprises.

Don Hutson received the most votes of any player, which was only natural since no one else could come close to him when comparing his impact on the team to theirs. At the other end position was Lavvie Dilweg who played eight years for Green Bay before going into politics. A distant third was Milt Gantenbein, which surprised many who were in the know. Gantenbein played 10 years for the Packers, four with Dilweg and six with Hutson. Local experts felt Milt was better than Hutson on defense and better than Dilweg on offense. To them, Gantenbein was the more complete player, whereas Hutson was strong on offense and Dilweg was tough on defense. Actually, Hutson's offensive prowess was so great that his defensive ability was overshadowed. The same was said about Dilweg's defense being so prominent that his offensive contributions were frequently overlooked. If the "All-Time" team was divided into defensive and offensive units, Gantenbein would have been chosen both ways, whereas Hutson would have been selected on offense only and Dilweg on defense only.

At the tackle positions, the fans chose Cal Hubbard and Cub Buck. Hubbard's selection was almost a foregone conclusion, the same as Hutson's had been. But the choice of Buck was a surprise in that he was an early player who had played in the days when most of the NFL comprised local elevens from more than two dozen small towns across mid-America. Ernie Smith finished third, but he was remembered more for his place-kicking talent than his blocking and tackling. Elmer Sleight from the '30 and '31 title teams came in a close fourth, and eight-year veteran Baby Ray was fifth. The vote counts for both of these men were surprising in that Sleight only played for the Packers those two years and Ray had been named to several all-league teams over his career to date.

The fans chose Mike Michalske and Buckets Goldenberg as the guards. Oddly, each man received the same number of votes, 1,738. Russ Letlow was a distant third with 251. The impressive fact about Goldenberg being chosen as a guard was, he had spent the first half of his career in the backfield as the blocking back in Lambeau's offensive scheme. Being a Wisconsin lad also played in Goldenberg's favor. Letlow was the better choice, but the war cut short his career by three years.

Charley Brock was the popular choice for center on the team. As a center on offense and a linebacker on defense, Brock was as good as they came in the NFL of that period. Jug Earpe was the runner-up, but he was only a center on offense. On defense, the Jugger played tackle.

The "All-Time" backfield had Arnie Herber at quarterback, Verne Lewellen and Johnny Blood at halfbacks, and Clarke Hinkle at fullback. Hinkle received only nine fewer votes than Hutson, which proved how much the fans of the day thought of him. Herber was named as the QB because he was a hometown boy and because of his legendary passing skills. Actually, Herber was a halfback most of the time. Lewellen was one of the few men of his day who could do it all: run, pass, catch, kick, block, and tackle. He was the complete football player. Blood was much like Lewellen in that he could do it all. His kicking and blocking weren't as good as Lewellen's, but his pass receiving and pass defending were better than Lewellen's. Furthermore, he was more colorful. Besides picking up 981 votes as quarterback, Herber also garnered 383 for halfback. Cecil Isbell polled 325 at half and 13 as QB. Red Dunn was named as the QB on 669 ballots.

The *Press-Gazette* poll was really unfair to the fans because it was asking them to pick the best players for *only* 11 positions. It would have better served Art Daley's purpose if he had realized that the Packers with Red Dunn and the Packers of all other years were two different animals. With Dunn at QB, Lambeau used the old Notre Dame "Box" formation, where the QB lined up a yard behind the center and took a *pass* from the lineman instead of a *snap*. After Dunn retired, Lambeau went to his own variation of the single-wing and double-wing attacks where the QB was actually a blocker who lined up a yard back of the space between the tackle and guard and the QB didn't handle the ball very much at all.

As a field general, Dunn was superior to any man who wore a Packer uniform to that time. For a blocking back, the choice would have to be made between Buckets Goldenberg and Larry Craig. For a passer, Cecil Isbell had the edge on Herber in that he was the better short and medium range passer, whereas Herber stood all alone as the best long passer in the history of the game.

For pure running backs, Lewellen, Blood, and Hinkle were the best in terms of service and production. Isbell was also a topnotch runner, and Tony Canadeo and Ted Fritsch were still showing their stuff. Andy Uram, Bobby Monnett, and Hank Bruder were three men whose contributions were somewhat overlooked by the voters.

Under Lambeau's usual defense, the Packers employed a six-man line with two or three men backing them and two halfbacks and a safety behind them. The lineup depended on who was in the game. Michalske and Russ Letlow were probably the two best defensive guards, Hubbard and Earpe the best defensive tackles, and Gantenbein and Dilweg the best defensive ends. For linebackers, Charley Brock and Clarke Hinkle were superior to all the rest. In the secondary, Blood, Lewellen, and Joe Laws, who had they played together in their primes, would have been an incredible trio.

For kicking specialists, Cub Buck was the best drop-kicker, Verne Lewellen the best punter, and Paul "Tiny" Engebretsen the best place-kicker.

All the members of the "All-Time" team except Cal Hubbard attended the "homecoming game" with the Cardinals in Green Bay as guests of the management, and joining them were the members of the 1919 Indian Packing Corporation football team. Art Daley called them the "first Green Bay Packer squad" in his *Sports Cocktails* column in the *Press-Gazette*. He wrote:

> It was composed of 20 young men, 19 of whom played football. The other gent was George W. Calhoun, present public relations chief who, at the time, handled the club's business affairs, passed the hat, counted the receipts and what not. The players were organized by Lambeau who wanted to play football so badly that he got backing from a local parking (sic) concern to buy the boys uniforms. How Curly got the club rolling and the headaches that developed are interesting indeed but for the sake of brevity tonight, let's discuss that first team which will be seated on the right of the Packer bench during the game.

Daley went on to update his readers on the whereabouts of the men who made up that team. The sports editor was personally acquainted with some of these men, which was evident by the little extra remarks he made about them in the column. One that he didn't know was Nate Abrams, of whom Daley wrote: "... one, Nate Abrams, died here several years ago." Nothing else was written about Abrams. Why? Daley couldn't remember why when he was interviewed for this book.

Besides the lack of words about Abrams, the other oddity was Daley's use of the word "several" in reference to the length of time since Abrams' death. Why? Especially why, since Abrams had passed away only five years before in 1941. Again, Daley couldn't recall a reason when he was interviewed.

Besides the typographical error that read "parking" instead of packing, the most curious line in the column was "How Curly got the club rolling ..." As stated in the first volume of *The History of the Green Bay Packers: The Lambeau Years, Part I*, Curly Lambeau *didn't* get "the club rolling" in the sense that Daley meant it. The team was already in place when Lambeau joined it in 1919. To reiterate earlier statements in that history, Lambeau pushed to have the annual team organizational meeting moved up because he was getting married and he didn't want to miss the meeting. When his teammates made him captain of the squad, he took it upon himself to arrange games for the team, using the occasion of his honeymoon to accomplish this. Daley never knew this, of course, because neither Lambeau nor Calhoun or any of the others who were around in 1919 told him those facts. All Daley knew at the time was the Packers were founded and coached by Earl L. "Curly" Lambeau in 1919 and that Lambeau's first team would be honored guests at the last home game of the 1946 season.

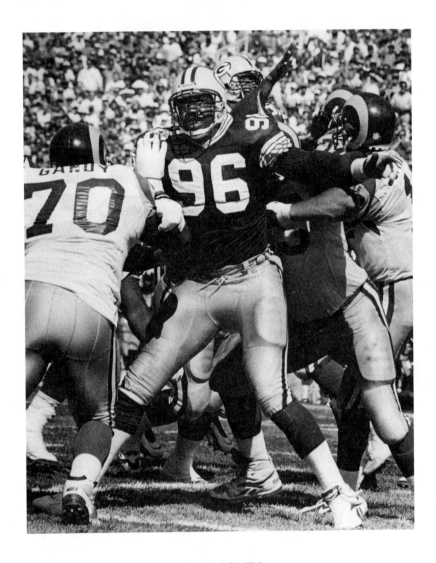

SEAN JONES

WHO REALLY OWNS THE PACKERS?

In the photo section of *The History of the Green Bay Packers, The Lambeau Years, Part Three* are pictures of three documents that are supposed to represent the same basic thing; i.e., a certificate of membership in the National Football League. Two are for the Green Bay Packers, while the other is for the Philadelphia Eagles. At a glance, one can easily see that two of the documents bare very little resemblance to the third. That is because those two are real, while the other is a very poor attempt at forgery.

The odd certificate for the Packers was copied from the sports pages of the November 9, 1945 issue of *The Green Bay Press-Gazette*. The real certificate for the Eagles was photocopied from the original which is in the library of the Professional Football Hall of Fame in Canton, Ohio. The real certificate for the Packers was photocopied from a photocopy on file at the same library.

The caption under the bogus Packer certificate read:

*Did you ever see this before? It is the franchise of the
Green Bay Packers in the National Football League. It was
issued in July 1935 and represents the transfer from the
Green Bay Football corporation to the Green Bay Packers,
Inc. Its value has been estimated by sports writers around the
country from $100,000 to $250,000. Lee Joannes, president
of the Green Bay Packers, Inc., declines to estimate its value.
He says: 'What is the difference how much it's worth, it's not
for sale and it is owned by a non-profit corporation? It cannot
be transferred without a majority vote of the 461 shares of
stock owned by 104 stockholders which would be practically
impossible to obtain because a comparatively small number
of the shareholders own more than one or two shares and
these are mostly manufacturing and mercantile business
concerns. It doesn't seem that any of these would vote to send
the Packers away from Green Bay.*

On February 2, 1950, while cleaning out his office at Packer
headquarters, Curly Lambeau was photographed removing the
certificate that granted him a franchise in the National Football
League from a file cabinet drawer. The caption said that the document
was dated June 24, 1922. Lambeau was quoted. He said jokingly,
"Say, I never did get my fifty dollars for that."

Following Lambeau's remark in the *Press-Gazette* was this
enclosed statement: "(The franchise was later turned over to the
corporation when the Packers were reorganized.)" Now why did Art
Daley go to all the trouble to make this point? Was there truth to the
rumor that Lambeau still owned the franchise?

Let's go back to 1921 and examine the facts.

The American Professional Football Association was begun in
1920 at a meeting in Canton, Ohio, of managers and owners of
professional teams. On August 27, 1921, the APFA granted a
franchise to John and Emmett Clair of the Acme Packing Company to
field a professional football team in Green Bay, Wisconsin. In a late
season game, the Packers employed three college players in a game.
When this was discovered and brought to the attention of Joe Carr, the

APFA president, a cry for blood went up. Emmett Clair attended the league meeting in January 1922. He made an apology for using the college players, and he voluntarily surrendered the franchise for Green Bay.

Unwilling to give up on professional football in Green Bay, Curly Lambeau attended the first APFA meeting held during the summer of 1922. He applied for a new franchise for Green Bay and was told he could have one providing he could come up with the fee for the franchise and pay $1,000 into the Guarantee Fund before September 1. Curly went back to Green Bay and found a backer, Nathan Abrams, who put up the money for the Guarantee Fund. Once the money was received by Joe Carr he issued a franchise certificate to E.L. Lambeau to operate a professional football team in Green Bay, Wisconsin. The certificate was signed at Dayton, Ohio, on August 21, 1922. It was signed by Carl L.H. Storck, and Joe F. Carr, secretary and president of the NFL, respectively.

Now that he had his franchise Lambeau and three friends, George Whitney Calhoun, Joe Ordens, and Nate Abrams, founded the Green Bay Football Club on September 8, 1922. They filed their incorporation papers with the secretary of state of Wisconsin on September 13, 1922, then registered them in Brown counties on September 14, 1922. (Certified copies of these papers are still on file at the Brown County Courthouse and at the corporation division of the secretary of state's office in Madison.)

Now that they were in business, they had stationery printed up that had some very interesting items on the letterhead.

TIME OUT:

A reproduction of the letterhead can be seen in the photo section of *The History of the Green Bay Packers, The Lambeau Years, Part Three* in a letter from Lambeau to Art Schmaehl.

TIME IN:

At the top of the letterhead was the rejoinder:

WISCONSIN PROFESSIONAL CHAMPIONS SINCE 1917

Note that (1) it didn't state that they were Wisconsin's *amateur* champions since 1917; (2) it didn't state that they were Wisconsin's professional champions *since 1919*, the mythical year that Curly Lambeau allegedly founded the Packers.

Below the credibility statement was the title of the business:

Green Bay Football Club

And beneath the title was another interesting item in small type and in parentheses:

Formerly Packers

This was Lambeau's attempt to dissociate his new franchise with the one that Emmett Clair had surrendered back in January. Because they were playing in blue and gold uniforms and because Calhoun had called them "the Big Bay Blues" in his column on occasion, Lambeau had opted to call his team the Green Bay Blues. The fans wouldn't let this name stick, however, because they knew Curly and most of the boys on the squad as the Packers.

To the left of the title, the executives were listed. Odd, but the offices weren't listed with the names of E.L. Lambeau, Nathan Abrams, and G.W. Calhoun. The text of the letter might hold a clue as to why they were listed without their official capacities. (Please note that I have not corrected Lambeau's spelling typos, but I have corrected the typewriter typos where words were run together. Also, I have italicized a few important parts of the letter.)

Sept. 17, 1922

Dear Friend Art:

We have a good team and are practicing every day. Buck, Murray, Moose Gardner, Owens, Nadolney constitutes our line with Dunnigan and Faye on ends. Our backfield is composed of Regnier of the Marines, Taugher and Cronin of Marquette, Davis and Chas. Mathys.

With exception of Mathys these fellows are playing for forty and fifty per game and living here. Now Art I want you to play here if possible. *I haven't it all to say* but I know I can get you 65 a game for you. If these figures are satisfactory please let me know at once. The management will not pay your transportation from Detroit.

There is a business man in town furnishing us all the money and he is the man that decides every money problem. He wants his name Kept out of Athletics or it would be made public.

Our first game is the 24th so we will have to rush things along.

With kindest personal regards,

(Signed) Curly

Curly stated that he wasn't in complete charge of things, and he wrote that a businessman in town was backing the team. The questions are simple: Who, besides Lambeau, had a say in running the team? Who was this businessman who wanted his name kept out of athletics? Obviously, Abrams and Calhoun had a say in the business of the Green Bay Football Club. So did Joe Ordens, as attested by the article written by Calhoun for a game program in 1946 that stated Ordens was part of the decision-making process when the management of the Packers was trying to decide whether to play the Thanksgiving Day game against the Duluth Kellys in 1922. The question is: Which of these three was the businessman that Lambeau mentioned in his letter to Art Schmaehl? Certainly not Calhoun the journalist. Possibly Ordens but not likely because he was a pencil pusher, not a financier. That only leaves Abrams who had been a businessman since he had started buying and selling cattle for a living at the age of 15. It was Abrams who helped Lambeau get his job with the Indian Packing Corporation in 1919, and it was Abrams who did a considerable amount of business with Lambeau's employer. Of the four incorporators of the Green Bay Football Club, Abrams was the only one who had the means to support the team.

The Packers played the 1922 season. Some really horrible weather and a less than stellar record kept the crowds down, and this hurt the club financially because they were bound by NFL rules to pay each visiting team a guarantee of $1,500 or 40% of the gate receipts (after stadium rental was deducted), depending on which figure was higher. If Lambeau's letter to Schmaehl is to be believed, the club was paying its players a total of about $1,000 per game. Other expenses mounted to the neighborhood of $1,000 per game. Just to break even on a home game, the club had to take in $3,500 in ticket sales. To do that, they had to sell all 2,000 tickets for prime seats at $1.65 each and an additional 500 tickets for end zone seats at $1.10 each. They failed to draw this many fans more than twice during the season.

TIME OUT:

See Chapter 6 of *The History of the Green Bay Packers, The Lambeau Years, Part One* for more about this crucial season in Packer history.

TIME IN:

The Green Bay Football Club was deep in debt when the 1922 season ended, but it wasn't out of business yet. The club, a legal entity itself, borrowed $3,000 from Nate Abrams to pay its bills. Abrams was given the franchise to hold as collateral.

Lambeau attended the January 1923 meeting of the NFL and had the name Green Bay Football Club placed over his name on his franchise certificate. As far as the NFL was concerned, he was still in business. He attended the summer meetings in July under the same pretext.

During the ensuing year, a new corporation was formed in Green Bay. The Green Bay Football Corporation was organized officially on August 14, 1923. Its incorporation papers were filed with the secretary of state on August 23, 1923. Certified copies of these papers are still on file at the Brown County Courthouse and at the corporation division of the secretary of state's office in Madison. In time, this new organization paid off the loan from Abrams, and he returned the franchise to Lambeau who gave his tacit approval to the Green Bay Football Corporation to handle the franchise. From this time forward, the National Football League franchise for the city of Green Bay, Wisconsin, has been *operated* by this corporation and its reorganized successor.

During the mid-1940s, rumors began to crop up that the Packers would be moved to a big city. Word had it that Lambeau still owned the franchise and that he planned to move it to Los Angeles or some other big city, possibly San Francisco. In an effort to squelch these tales, Ray Pagel, sports editor of the *Press-Gazette* was given a photograph of a phony franchise certificate by someone, which he printed in the newspaper, thinking nothing was wrong with it.

TIME OUT:

Most likely this someone was Andy Turnbull, top man at the *Press-Gazette*. Lee Remmel, who was a reporter for the newspaper at that time, related that Turnbull had a policy of printing nothing derogatory about Lambeau or the Packers' management. Turnbull was still the big power behind Lambeau and the Packers until his retirement from the Packers' corporation in 1948.

TIME IN:

The importance of the photo wasn't so much the certificate but the caption which attempted to convince readers that the Packers couldn't be shifted to another city without permission of the stockholders and that wasn't likely to happen. The picture of the certificate was meant to reinforce the denial that Lambeau still had the franchise in his possession.

The photo of the certificate was published on November 9, 1945. This was a Friday. Lambeau was out of town with the team and on the way to Cleveland by the time the newspaper hit the newsstands. Could it be that Pagel deliberately waited until Lambeau was out of town and was unlikely to see the picture at all, especially since he would be absent from Green Bay for more than three weeks? Yes.

To silence the chatter once and for all, Lambeau was given a new contract after the Cleveland game on November 11, 1945. All was

quiet for a couple of years before the series of events that led to
Lambeau's resignation began.

TIME OUT:
    See Chapter 18, page 231 of *The History of the Green Bay
Packers, The Lambeau Years Part Two* for more about this incident.

TIME IN:
    When push came to shove between Lambeau and the executive
committee again in 1949, the rumors flew anew. The most prominent
of these had Lambeau and Vic McCormick preparing to take over the
corporation and reorganizing it into a profit-sharing business.
Lambeau even made this proposition public before that fateful board
of directors meeting in late November. To divert Lambeau once again
from making a move on the franchise, the board voted to renew
Lambeau's contract for two years.
    Lambeau felt that he had won the battle with Jerry Clifford and
discarded his plans to gain control of the corporation and reorganize
it. Then Emil Fischer met him at the winter meeting in Philadelphia
and presented him with a contract that was unacceptable. Instead of
renewing the fight, Lambeau packed up and left Green Bay for the
Chicago Cardinals, taking the franchise certificate with him.
    Although Lambeau was gone, the question of whether he still
owned the franchise persisted in popping up. That point became moot
in 1963 when Lambeau turned over the franchise certificate to the
Green Bay Packers, Inc.
    More than one person who knew Lambeau personally related that
he was a known liar; "an inveterate liar," said one; "an incorrigible
liar," said another. But he did tell the truth on occasion, such as those
times when he was quoted more than once as saying that he didn't
own the franchise. He did own a franchise certificate of membership
in the NFL, but that certificate only granted him the right to field a
team in Green Bay, Wisconsin, to play in the NFL for the 1922
season.
    All of this business of who owned the franchise was actually
superfluous. On the day that Lambeau gave his permission for the

Green Bay Football Club to operate his franchise, he began to surrender any claim to ownership of the Green Bay Packers football team. To complicate matters further, the Green Bay Football Club then allowed the Green Bay Football Corporation to operate the franchise in 1923, and it passed the baton to its successor, the Green Bay Packers, Inc., in 1935. None of these changes of command were registered with the NFL, but they took place all the same. These unofficial transfers of the franchise made each corporation that operated the team after Lambeau was granted a franchise *de facto owners* of the Green Bay Packers.

Who owns the Packers? Why, the fans, of course. Who else could?

MIKE HOLMGREN

THE NEW CITY STADIUM

In early 1954, a letter addressed to the Packers and the city of Green Bay from the Sullivan-Wallen American Legion Post in Green Bay and printed in the *Press-Gazette* recommended that some consideration be given to construction of a new stadium and suggested that rental fees from each game be placed in a trust fund and used to build onto the stadium in later years as the need would arise. This was the first official thought given to building a new playing facility, but more about this subject later.

Art Daley wrote a story about the need for a new stadium and what it would take to get one. He listed three things that had to happen before Green Bay could get another playground for its Packers.

(1) Winning seasons or the right kind of team.
(2) Sellout crowds at games in City Stadium.
(3) Milwaukee outdrawing Green Bay to the extent that

other teams will put pressure on the Packers to play in Milwaukee rather than in Green Bay.

Thing No. 1 is an absolute must because if the Packers have a winner that will draw tremendously on the road—due to their natural small-town appeal and their power on the field ... drawing on the road would skyrocket the club's finances since it would easily wipe out the tremendous expense of traveling. Large crowds at home, drawn by that must—a good team—would thicken the stadium-building gravy.

Thing No. 2 represents the above-mentioned Joe Phan. He must demonstrate the need for a larger stadium in Green Bay. With few exceptions, the fans annually leave a number of empty seats during league games.

Last fall, for instance, only one game in City Stadium was a sellout—24,835 at the Bear go. The Detroit test drew 20,834, and Baltimore pulled in 18,713. These figures do not show a need for a new and larger stadium.

Thing No. 3 is the key ...

Every year ... George Halas of the Bears puts pressure on the Packers to move his game to Milwaukee. Halas figures the Packers owe him something for the large checks they've been hauling out of Wrigley Field every fall. He wants to get a few of those checks back out of the spacious Milwaukee stadium.

Daley pointed out that other teams were also putting pressure on the Packers to move their games to Milwaukee in order to get a bigger payout from the gate and to avoid the extra expense of traveling to Green Bay. These clubs had a legitimate gripe, and the Packers knew it. Daley's article made sense, and the fans knew it. The move for a new stadium was now underway.

In June, the Green Bay city council plunked down $500 for an eight-month option on a 40-acre tract on the city's west side located between Military Avenue and Platten Street and bordered on the south by Boland Road. The owner of this land was Mrs. George Morrow who stated she was willing to accept a down payment of $30,000 and the balance of $28,000 to be paid to her over 25 years at 4% or 4.5% interest. The council's original thoughts were to offer Mrs. Morrow a $2,000-option for six months, but they opted for the longer term at less money because they wanted to give the state legislature time to pass a bill that would allow the Brown County government to become involved in the project.

Adding spice to the stadium project was the will of Dr. Clarence Delmarcelle. City Attorney Clarence Nier reported that the stadium could be financed in part by the late doctor's estate. Delmarcelle's will stated that the city was to receive the residue of his estate after all the beneficiaries were deceased and further stated that construction of a new stadium on the city's west side had to begin within one year after the demise of the last beneficiary. Nier reported that the beneficiaries ranged in age from 55 to 76 years old and that the city's share of the estate stood at $235,901.46 as of that day, June 14, 1954.

With the off-season after the '54 campaign came more talk about a new stadium for the Packers or at least a renovation of the present City Stadium. In January 1955, Russ Bogda submitted a report to the Green Bay City Park Board stating the Packers would participate in the expense of a feasibility study on the expansion of City Stadium seating to 30,000 or even 32,000. The Packers even offered to help pay for the additional seats out of ticket sales. Bogda's report pointed out how some NFL opponent's preferred playing in Milwaukee over Green Bay for two reasons: larger seating capacity at Milwaukee County Stadium and lower travel costs to the Cream City. Although the report didn't say so, George Halas wanted to play the Packers in Milwaukee instead of Green Bay because more Chicago fans could attend the game and that meant more money for both teams. Of course, the fans in Green Bay would never permit that to happen. The answer was a new stadium or at the very least a renovated old City Stadium.

The Green Bay City Council took Bogda's report under consideration, and Mayor Dominic Olejniczak, also a member of the executive committee, invited Bogda and the rest of the executive committee to attend a January 17 meeting of the council where the council intended to discuss the feasibility of replacing the wooden seats at City Stadium with steel seats and expanding capacity to 30,000-32,000. Olejniczak stated that the increased seating plan would help the Packers at the NFL scheduling meeting on January 27, meaning league opponents might be more receptive to playing in Green Bay during the coming season.

The January 17 council meeting resulted in the hiring of an architect to prepare plans and make a cost estimate of expanding the current City Stadium and replacing the old wooden benches with steel ones. Bogda told the council that renovating the old stadium was a better choice fiscally. "The big need is for added seats," he said. The reasons? "First, because we think we can fill them and, second, because it is increasingly difficult to schedule games here." His report stated City Stadium's 25,000 capacity limit compared with Milwaukee County Stadium put the club at a considerable handicap in scheduling games in Green Bay and the situation was becoming "more embarrassing as time goes by. For example, there isn't any question that 42,000 seats would be sold if the Bear game were played in Milwaukee or that the same would be true if Green Bay had that many seats."

Adding fuel to Bogda's fire, Building Inspector Al Manders said that maintenance costs of the present wooden stadium were increasing and "the time for replacing two-thirds of the stadium isn't too far off."

The only opposition to the council's action was voiced by Alderman Leonard Jahn who advocated a new stadium at the Military Avenue and Boland Road site, which the council ordered bought for a future park or arena. Jahn called the enlarging of City Stadium "near sighted" and predicted that the present stadium could never be expanded above 35,000 seats if the need should arise. He said the people of Green Bay would rather see a new stadium with plenty of parking space and asked if the Packers had considered the parking factor in their report.

Bogda replied with a lot of possibilities, such as parking on the sites of older homes in the area, constructing a foot bridge across the East River from a park on the eastern bank, and the probability that the University Extension Center might move from its present Baird Street location making it available for parking.

Alderman Robert Bittner labeled Jahn's criticism as "unfair" in light of the complete report from the Packers which he said considered all factors. Evidently, Mr. Bittner knew where to put his lips.

The architecture firm that the city hired was Foeller, Schober, Berners, Safford, and Jahn. Ed Berners presented two plans to the Green Bay board of education in August: one with a track running around the field and one without. The board approved the plan with the track because City Stadium was located at East High School and the young athletes of Green Bay would still need a running course for track in the spring. The new seating capacity would be increased to approximately 32,000, and this pleased the Packers, although Fred Leicht, chair of the stadium committee, said the corporation preferred the plan without the track. Leicht described the proposed new stadium as the best in professional football because of all the sideline seats, over 22,000, but he seemed to forget that the Rams played in the Los Angeles Coliseum, which had more than 40,000 seats on its sidelines.

A couple of weeks later Alderman Jahn made a report on the proposed renovation of City Stadium to the Green Bay Traffic Commission, and he received instant backing for his opposition to the project. Jahn read Green Bay's General Ordinance Number 30-54, part of which read:

> *No stadium, ball park, or other sports arena shall be con-structed unless one parking space is provided for every five seats in the stadium. Said parking area or any portion thereof*

*shall not be more than 800 feet to the nearest corner of the
property on which the place of assembly (stadium) is located.*

City attorney Clarence Nier said a determination would have to be
made whether the city government's functions would be bound by the
ordinance and whether the City Stadium improvement would be
classified as a new structure subject to the ordinance.

The new stadium advocates countered with another part of the
ordinance that supported their case. The clause provided for capacity
increases in current assembly sites, stating that if parking potential
should be increased by 15% the requirements of the ordinance become
effective. Adding 7,000 new seats would require 1,400 new parking
spaces, an increase of 28%.

Taking this into account, commission chairman Charles
McFarland said:

*"We should tell the council that we consider it definitely
out of line to spend thousands and thousands of dollars on a
new stadium at the present site when there is no chance in the
world of improving the traffic and parking situation out
there."*

Jahn continued his salvo by pointing out all the positives for
building a new stadium at the Military Avenue and Boland Road site,
now called E.J. Perkins Park. He remarked on costs of construction
and the accessibility of the locality to automobile traffic. He presented
numbers to support the former line argument, and Lt. Harry Bultman
of the Green Bay Police Department Traffic Division agreed with the
latter when he offered his opinions as well as some facts on the
controversy. "It goes without saying that the job of the police
department would be even tougher than it is now," said Bultman.

More than a month passed before the Green Bay City Council
hired architect John Somerville to do a cost study comparing the

expense of renovating old City Stadium and building a new one at Perkins Park. Somerville came up with a figure of $960,000 for a new stadium, which wasn't much more than the cost of remodeling the old stadium at East High. His study swung a majority of people to Jahn's side of the argument for a new stadium.

In January 1956, Curly Lambeau put in his two cents about the stadium situation in Green Bay. His observations made some good sense, which made them suspect by many people of the area. Born and raised on the east side of Green Bay, having attended East High School, and having played and coached the Packers in stadiums that were all located on the east side of the Fox River, it would only be natural for Lambeau to favor remodeling City Stadium, but he took the opposite stance. "That super highway is a temptation for fans in Milwaukee, south of there, and in the valley to come (here)," he said. "Same for fans coming from north and west (of here)." In other words, placing a new stadium on the west side near U.S. Highway 41 would make it more accessible to out of town fans. Practical and wise—and from Lambeau! What a shock!

In March, the ball rolling toward the construction of a new stadium was given a little more momentum with the formation of a group called "Citizens Committee for the Stadium" or CCFTS as Art Daley tagged it in the *Press-Gazette*. Heading up this bunch were Tony Canadeo and Jerry Atkinson, and actively supporting the movement for a new stadium were Green Bay's new mayor, Otto Rachals, and former mayor and current corporation vice-president Dominic Olejniczak. At the heart of their immediate efforts was the bond issue that would be on the April 3 ballot. If approved by the voters, Green Bay—and the Packers—would soon begin building a new City Stadium. They presented the argument that it would only cost each citizen of Green Bay 50 cents a year for the next 20 years to pay for the new stadium. This was based on the cost to the city of $600,000, including the interest on the bonds over that time period, divided by an average population of 60,000 over the next two decades.

Put in those terms, the stadium was a real bargain.

Art Daley did his part to support the drive for a new stadium. He wrote a series of articles on the history of the Packers, and for the most part, he told the story in very general terms, hitting the highlights and avoiding the less savory moments completely. When he did get specific, he more often than not had the wrong information, such as when he perpetuated the myth that Lambeau founded the Packers all by himself. Some founder! Young Curly failed to show up at the very first organizational meeting back in 1919, a fact overlooked by Daley in his story on the so-called founding meeting. By the way, Nate Abrams, the guy who started and ran the town team the year before in 1918, did attend the first meeting of the town team in 1919 and there is reason to believe that he organized the meeting in the first place.

The outside world took notice of the upcoming election in Green Bay. *Associated Press* writer Chuck Capaldo wrote:

> *The future of the Green Bay Packers' unique, 37-year relationship with this city of 50,000 hinges on a referendum on the April 3 ballot.*
>
> *Voters will be asked whether the city—smallest of the ten with the National Football League franchises—should float a $960,000 bond issue to finance a new stadium for use by the Packers and the city's schools.*
>
> *But, one fact is sure. If the question doesn't win voter approval the Packers will pull up stakes within the next few years and move elsewhere. Possible future sites of the club include Milwaukee, Buffalo, N.Y., and Miami, Fla., and Minneapolis.*

Except for the fact that the NFL was located in 11 cities, not just 10, Capaldo hit the nail on the head. No stadium, no Packers in Green Bay. That was the bottom line. Richard McFarland of *United Press International* quoted Mayor Rachals as saying:

*"A victory is vital to keeping the Packers in Green
Bay."*

Holy flyin' footballs, Batman! This stadium thing was getting
serious. More serious than many people thought in the beginning.
Thus, the reason for mentioning publicly in the newspapers that Green
Bay was in danger of losing the Packers if the voters turned down the
bond issue. This was no scare tactic to pressure the voters. This was
for real. Many NFL owners wanted the franchise moved to a bigger
city with a bigger stadium, and some of them who could see past today
wanted it in a bigger television market. This called for drastic
measures.

A few days before the election the CCFTS called out three big
guns to speak at a rally supporting the bond issue. With Tony Canadeo
acting as master of ceremonies, Curly Lambeau, Johnny (Blood)
McNally, and none other than George Halas spoke to an audience of
nearly 1,000 people gathered at the Columbus Club in Green Bay.
Each of them was quoted in the *Press-Gazette*.

Lambeau: "The Packer franchise could be sold for a
million dollars in 24 hours."

Halas: "Buffalo is ready to doubledeck its 32,000 (seat)
stadium at a cost of a million dollars if it can get a franchise."

McNally: "Minneapolis is ready, willing, and able to take
over the Packer franchise. Minneapolis is just finishing a new
stadium."

Translation: If you don't vote YES on Tuesday, say good-bye to
the Packers on Wednesday.

The day before the election Verne Lewellen addressed the local
Kiwanis Club luncheon, and he made a prediction. He said:

*"I firmly believe the golden era is going to be in the
1960's."*

Now that's a real prognostication. Maybe it was only wishful
thinking, but Lewellen explained his thoughts by predicting crowds of
35,000-45,000 and television audiences of 50 million and more. This
was a positive attitude that hadn't been shown up all that well until
this moment. Possibly, Lewellen's rosy painting of the future had an
influence on the voters because when all the ballots were counted the
bond issue passed by more than a two-to-one margin. Green Bay
would have a new stadium, and the Packers would remain where they
belonged—forever!

Now that the money was guaranteed the Packers engaged the
Osborn Engineering Company of Cleveland to make a complete
survey and report on the best site for a new city stadium in Green Bay.
This move was not exactly within the purview of the corporation; this
function belonged to the city council. Bogda stated:

> *Since this new stadium is so important to the future of the
> Packers here, and since we are paying for half of it, we feel
> it is absolutely essential that all of the facts regarding the
> location of the stadium should be developed and studied. The
> Osborn company is recognized as the top authority in the
> nation on stadium matters, and we feel that a complete study
> by an independent firm of this type is a must.*
>
> *None of us on the executive committee are experts in this
> field and we want the advice of the best experts in the country
> when we are going to spend this kind of money.*

Osborn Engineering was the same firm that had done the study
and made the selection for Milwaukee County Stadium. The
company's other credits included work for Notre Dame, Purdue,
Indiana University, the University of Michigan, the University of

Minnesota, Municipal Stadium in Cleveland, the Rubber Bowl in Akron, Yankee Stadium, Briggs Stadium in Detroit, the Polo Grounds, Griffith Stadium in Washington, and several others. In other words, their credentials were impeccable.

On July 10, 1956, the Osborn company reported to the city council that Green Bay's new stadium should be built at the southeast corner of Highland Avenue and Ridge Road, part of Ashwaubenon. This stunned just about everybody in Green Bay, especially the proponents of building the new stadium in Perkins Park. The firm also reported that parking space there would cost less than at either old City Stadium or Perkins Park. The figures also favored the new site. The cost of a new stadium with 20,000 permanent seats and 12,000 bleacher seats would be $947,000 at the Highland-Ridge location, $986,000 at Perkins Park, and $1,017,000 for rebuilding City Stadium. In addition to the cost of the stadium, the land had to be purchased and the amount necessary for parking had to be added. The land and parking at the Highland-Ridge site would be $79,500 and $50,000 for a total of $129,500. To provide enough parking at Perkins Park, another $175,000 would be needed, and the land would cost yet another $75,000. The additional land needed for sufficient parking at old City Stadium wasn't included because it was felt that renovation of the stadium was no longer a viable alternative.

Besides the dollars and cents, the report listed the advantages and disadvantages for all three sites.

City Stadium

Advantages: Land city-owned with field and track already installed; nearness for use by East High School; and convenience to downtown civic events.

Disadvantages: Poor foundation with resulting higher costs and hazardous to present high school building which adjoins the new work; extremely limited opportunity for off-street parking; restricted access from out of town because of narrow streets and few main traffic arteries; and little or no space for future stadium expansion.

<u>Perkins Park</u>
   Advantages: Land city owned and cleared; adequate parking area could be purchased; favorable topography and foundation; and ample expansion space.
   Disadvantages: Limited access to present through streets and silty soil surface requiring added costs for surfacing parking area.

<u>Highland-Ridge Site</u>
   Advantages: Good soil; good topography; good access to major highway and through streets; no additional costs to provide parking space.
   Disadvantages: Land privately owned, and all construction would be from scratch.

   Only the two aldermen who represented districts near the current City Stadium raised objections to the report. Alderman Rhynie Dantinne questioned whether the Osborn report was in keeping with a location near the population center of Green Bay, and he revived the subject of building a foot bridge across the East River to be used by fans who parked on the east side of the river. Dantinne and Alderman Clarence Vandermus were clearly thinking of their own political futures rather than the future of Green Bay and the Packers.
   When the city council voted on the Osborn report the following week, only seven of the 24 aldermen voted against the Highland-Ridge location. They were Tim De Wane, Eddie Bodart, Clarence Vandermus, Rhynie Dantinne, Clarence Deschamps, Robert Baye, and Don Tilleman. All of these men represented districts east of the Fox River, and all of them put their own constituencies ahead of the good of the city. This was the typical thinking of the common political hack.

Besides approving the site, the council voted the same way on a four-step proposal by Mayor Rachals before construction could begin.

1. Purchase of the 53-acre site on a three-year term basis with a down payment of $26,000 to be advanced by the Packer corporation as part of its pledge to pay half the $960,000 bond issue over 20 years.

2. Directing the Board of Public Works to pick an architect to draw stadium plans with alternatives to make as certain as possible that total cost would fall within the bond issue.

3. Instructing the city attorney to start work toward sale of the $960,000 bond issue approved in the April referendum.

4. Obtaining a contract with the Packers for its half of the bond issue to pledge the corporation's assets to the fullest extent legally possible.

In October, the city council voted to pay $70,000 for the excavating that was necessary to shape the site into a bowl. This move allowed the construction of the stadium to begin before the bond issue was completed. The Department of Public Works would do the job for much less than the lowest bid submitted by a private contractor. The earth movers began their task on October 11, 1956, and hoped to be done before the frost set in.

Although the excavating went along smoothly, the money situation didn't. The architect, John Somerville, told the stadium planning committee that his current (October 25) estimate for the stadium, after dropping alternatives from his plans, was about $995,000, a good $35,000 over the bond issue approved in the April election. If the stadium was to be built with all the construction hoped for in the tentative drawings, the total cost would be $228,000 over the bond limit, but Somerville had come up with alternatives that would lower that amount by $193,400. The largest and most important of

Somerville's alternatives was changing the seating from 24,000 permanent seats and 8,000 bleacher seats to 20,000 permanent seats and 12,000 bleacher seats as was originally proposed. The real kicker was the work and materials needed for the parking area. This cost was not included in Somerville's estimate. This was a real snag.

The city council voted to accept Somerville's proposal to cut permanent seating to 20,734 and increase the bleacher seats to approximately 12,000. Also, they chose to reduce the size of the proposed press box and make some building materials changes in the other structures which would reduce costs. By the time all these cuts were made, the total price for the new stadium stood at $939,200. With the figures now fitting the budget, target dates for the finished construction plans and the opening of bids were set. The former was December 1, and the latter was January 1, 1957.

By January 21, 1957, all the bids had been received, and much to the City Council's delight, all of them came in under the amount allotted for the construction of the new stadium. The question remained whether the new facility would have 32,026 permanent seats of steel construction or 23,490 permanent seats of concrete construction and 9,792 bleacher seats made of wood and steel.

A week later the contract to build the new stadium was awarded to George Hougard and Son, Inc., of Green Bay. The deal included a completion date of September 15, 1957, just in time for the Bears and Packers to open the '57 playing season. The final plan called for 32,026 permanent seats of concrete construction at a cost of $742,039. Each sideline would have 11,745 seats in 25 rows, while the end zones would each have 4,268 seats in 21 rows. Building all the seats with steel or making only the sideline seats permanent with concrete and the end zone seats with wood and steel would have been cheaper, but delivery of the steel needed for the job couldn't be guaranteed in time to assure the completion date of September 15. Thus, the City Council opted to go with all concrete seating. It proved to be a wise decision.

The following week the Green Bay Packers, Inc., and the City of

Green Bay agreed to a 21-year lease of the new stadium that called for the Packers to pay the city $30,000 a year. This was how the Packers would pay for their half of the construction costs, and as a bonus, the Packers were given an option of continuing the lease for another 10 years under the same terms. This was a real deal for the Packers.

Now the problem of parking. The county government had the idea of making a single parking lot for the new stadium and the new arena that was being built across Oneida Street. The county gave up land to make this possible, and that more or less removed the question marks about parking space. Now all they had to do was pay for it. To do that, the city borrowed $150,000 from local banks.

With construction well begun by the fourth week of March, a dedication date of September 29 was announced by Tony Canadeo and Jerry Atkinson, designated by Mayor Rachals as co-chairmen of a citizens dedication committee. This was quite appropriate because the Packers would be opening the '57 campaign that day against their arch rival, the hated Chicago Bears.

In April, the City Council created a five-seat commission to administer the stadium. The president of this body was Clarence Nier, the city attorney. Ronald McDonald was made vice-president, and Fred Leicht from the Packer corporation was designated secretary. The other two commissioners were Jerome Quinn and Robert Baye, Green Bay aldermen.

In May, the construction moved into a new phase right on schedule. The contractor would begin erecting the steel beams that were to hold up the seats above the ground, starting with the west side of the stadium. At the same time, the team building, i.e., locker room, offices, visitors dressing room, would be started. The playing field was now dry enough to begin the laying of sod, and the sideline areas would be seeded as soon as the gridiron was completed.

Everything seemed to be going well until the carpenters went on strike when the contract between the Carpenters Local No. 1146 and the Fox River Valley Construction Association expired on the first of

June. Hoping for a quick settlement, the carpenters placed no pickets around the stadium construction site, which allowed the other unions to continue their work there, but contractor George Hougard stated unequivocally that it wouldn't be long until the other workers would have to stop work as well until the carpenters returned to the job. He was right. Within two weeks, the rest of the men working on the stadium could go no further with their tasks without the carpenters.

Hougard sat squarely on the horns of a dilemma. His company was a member of the Fox River Valley Construction Association, and he could do nothing unilaterally without suffering the wrath of his fellow contractors. On the other hand, he had a deadline to meet with the construction of the stadium. To delay the job beyond the two weeks that had already lapsed would put the completion date in serious jeopardy. Fortunately, he had anticipated the strike and had set up his construction schedule to have the stadium completed by September 1 instead of the September 15 deadline as the contract stipulated. Hougard could ride with the FRVCA and risk finishing the stadium after the deadline or he could buck the system and make his own deal with the union.

Hougard did what was best for everyone involved except his fellow contractors. He signed a separate agreement with the union, agreeing to pay the carpenters 25 cents an hour more, and the carpenters went back to work on June 17. For doing the right thing, Hougard was ousted from the Green Bay Building Trades Employers Association by his fellow contractors.

The rest of the contractors settled with the union a week later, agreeing to a raise of 50 cents an hour which was spread out over three years: 20 cents the first year and 15 cents an hour for the second and third years. The deal Hougard cut with the carpenters was better for them, so he stuck to it. This was an honorable man building the new stadium.

As part of the overall change in playing venue for the Packers, a new practice facility was platted across Oneida Street from the new stadium. The Packers began practicing there on September 17, 1957, which marked the first time in the history of professional football in Green Bay, whether as the Packers or the town team that preceded them, that the local heroes practiced or played on the west side of the Fox River in Green Bay. To those people who failed to recognize how Green Bay had become a small metropolis by this time, the move was as momentous as the Brooklyn Dodgers and New York Giants moving their franchises to the West Coast later that year.

The stadium was finally completed and in time for the opening of the 1957 season. A whole celebration was planned to mark the event, and Mother Nature co-operated with near-perfect early autumn weather.

A parade began at Ashland Avenue and West Walnut and proceeded to old City Stadium where television actor James Arness, who portrayed Marshal Matt Dillon in the TV series *Gunsmoke,* and Miss America, Marilyn Elaine Van Derbur, were entertaining the crowd waiting there. The procession consisted of six marching sections, each with bands, variety acts, and interspersed with 35 floats for the occasion. The ceremonies at the old stadium concluded with the lowering of the flag to mark the end of professional football there. Then a Venetian Night with spectacular fireworks and a flotilla of lighted boats on the Fox River illumined the evening. The crowds were estimated at 70,000 for the parade; 18,000 for the festivities at the old stadium; and another 15,000 for the Venetian Night.

Before the game on Sunday, Green Bay's mayor, Otto Rachals, opened the ceremonies with a dedication speech. Then he introduced members of the City Council, City Attorney Clarence Nier, City Engineer F. J. Euclide, and Roman Denissen, his 1957 mayoralty opponent and former Council president. Rachals paid tribute to the late First Ward Alderman Harold Reynolds, and he praised architect John Somerville and contractor George Hougard. Nier, as Stadium Commission president, took a turn speaking, then a brief prayer was offered by the Rev. Anselm Keefe. The Packer Band then played the

National Anthem as the flag was raised over the stadium to begin a new era in Packer football history. At half-time, Wisconsin Governor Vernon W. Thomson was the first speaker. In turn, he was followed by Congressman John Byrnes, NFL Commissioner Bert Bell, George Halas, and Vice-President Richard M. Nixon. Master of ceremonies Dominic Olejniczak read a telegram from Curly Lambeau, and he introduced Gene Ronzani and Marilyn Van Derbur.

To cap off a perfect weekend, the Packers showed their appreciation for the new plant, which was considered to be the best in the NFL at the time and in decades to come. Of the 12 teams in the league in 1957, Green Bay had the only stadium that was strictly an arena for football. Every other team played in a baseball park or a stadium that was constructed for track and field events, such as the Los Angeles Coliseum. The Packers played in the smallest town in the league, but on the best field. Incredible! But that was Green Bay.

PACKER CHRONOLGY

T he best way to put the history of a team in perspective is to put it in order, in chronological order, meaning from the beginning to the present. With the Packers, this is difficult because of the controversies surrounding the team's genesis. Do we start with the formal birth of the Green Bay Football Club, Inc., when Curly Lambeau was granted a franchise to field a professional football team in the city of Green Bay, Wisconsin, to play in the National Football League? Do we start with the first year the city of Green Bay had a professional team in the NFL? Do we start with the first year that the town team was known as the Packers? Or do we start with beginning of professional football in Green Bay, Wisconsin, which would mean going all the way back to 1896? Tough choice. Let's go for the last one because that would better serve the Packers and their fans who are so proud of the tradition that goes deeper into history than any other team in professional football.

1895 - Fred Hulbert starts the very first professional town team in recorded and reported Green Bay football history. As reported in the *Green Bay Gazette* October 19, 1895, the Green Bay town team played the Stevens Point Normal school in Stevens Point and got taught a serious lesson in football, 48-0. The newspaper reported the lineup as

> F. (Frank) Hurlbut, Jr., left end; E. Neuschwander, left tackle; J. (Joseph) Jackson, left guard; A. Hiller, center; J. (John) Gray, right guard; F. (Frank) Flatley, right tackle; B. (Bert) Banzhof, right end; A. Clements, quarterback; J. (John) Thomas, left halfback; D. (Dandy) Davis, right halfback; Fred Hulbert, fullback and captain. E. Challenger and D. Shyer went as substitutes, and H. Cotton went as umpire, while the position of manager will be filled by Will Sheehy.

In later years, Hulbert would call the team the Athletics in newspaper advertising.

1896 - Joseph Miller quarterbacked, captained, and coached the second Green Bay town team that passed the hat during the games to collect a little money for the boys on the field.

1897 - Tom Skenandore, a legendary athlete of native American extraction, was paid to play for the Green Bay town team to become the first really professional player to play in Green Bay.

1900 - Ralph Glynn was the first player from Notre Dame to play for Green Bay.

1917 - Green Bay failed to field a town football team for the first time in 21 years as most young athletes of fighting age enlist or are drafted into the Army and Navy to serve in World War I. A city league continued to play, and an all-star team from that circuit represented Green Bay in a late-season contest against a local military eleven.

1918 - Nate Abrams, a local young businessman and sportsman, financed the town team, which was nicknamed the Whales after the Chicago Whales of the now defunct Federal League of Major League Baseball. Curly Lambeau didn't play on this team because he was playing beside the legendary George Gipp at Notre Dame.

1919 - George Whitney Calhoun, sports editor for the Green Bay *Press-Gazette*, called for a meeting of "footballers" to organize the town football team for that year. The meeting was held in the editorial office of the newspaper on August 11. Curly Lambeau wasn't in attendance, so no decisions were made at that time. Calhoun called for a second meeting to be held two nights later, and this time he named the players who had missed the first meeting. Lambeau's name was not among the truant, but he did attend the meeting at the personal insistence of Calhoun who talked him out of going back to college at Notre Dame in favor of playing for the town team. Voted to be the team's captain and leader, Lambeau obtained financial backing from his employer, the Indian Packing Corporation, and the team took the nickname of Packers. Like so many Green Bay town teams before them, the Packers defeated all comers on their schedule, but they lost their last game, a challenge affair for a mythical state championship, to the Fairbanks-Morse eleven from Beloit.

1920 - Green Bay town team continued to be sponsored by the local packing company, now named the Acme Packing Company. Lambeau was again voted to be the team's captain, and the Packers roll over all opponents except Fairbanks-Morse team from Beloit and an aggregation known as the Chicago Boosters. Packers split with Beloit eleven in two games and earned a tie with the Boosters.

1921 - Representing John and Emmett Clair, executives of the Acme Packing Company, Lambeau attended the summer meeting of the fledgling professional football league, and he obtained a franchise in the National Football League for them to field a team in Green Bay, Wisconsin.

- October 23, the Packers played their first game in the NFL, defeating the Minneapolis Marines, 7-6, in Green Bay.

- November 20, the Packers made their first trip to Chicago to play the big city boys, and they managed a tie against the Cardinals.

- November 27, the Packers spent another Sunday in Chicago and lost to the Chicago Staleys, 20-0. In years to come, the NFL officially determined this game to be the beginning of the Packers-Bears series. In this game, Lambeau used some college players whose seasons were already completed.

1922 - At the January meeting of the NFL, league officials, at the urging and insistence of George Halas, demanded the surrender of the Green Bay franchise because Lambeau had used college players in a league game, and Emmett Clair returned the franchise to the league.

- August 22, the NFL officially granted a franchise to E.L. Lambeau to field a team in Green Bay.

- September 8, Lambeau, Nate Abrams, George Whitney Calhoun, and Joe Ordens formed the Green Bay Football Club, Inc., to operate the franchise granted to Lambeau.

- November 5, a heavy rain fell before the game, and Lambeau, Abrams, Calhoun, and Ordens wanted to cancel the contest against the Columbus Panhandles. Joe Carr, the owner of the Columbus team and also the president of the NFL, advised the Packer owners to play the game or risk losing their franchise. The game was played; Packers won, 3-0; but the Packers lost a lot of money on it.

- November 30, Thanksgiving Day, hoping to save themselves from financial disaster, Lambeau, Abrams, Calhoun, and Ordens scheduled an extra game, a non-league affair with the Duluth Kellys. An all-night rain and threatening skies an hour before kickoff forced them to confer about whether to play or not. If they play, attendance probably won't cover the guarantee to Duluth. If they don't play, pro football will most likely die in Green Bay. While debating the issue, they were visited by Andrew Turnbull, the business manager of the Green Bay *Press-Gazette*, and he advised them to play the game and take their losses in order to save pro football for the city. They played the game; won, 10-0; lost money; but saved the franchise.

1923 - Turnbull organized a meeting of businessmen and community leaders, and attorney Gerald Clifford provided the legal work for the founding of the Green Bay Football Corporation. Enough stock was bought by the citizens of the area to pay off the debts incurred by Lambeau and friends, and Turnbull was elected president of the new corporation that assumed operation of the Packers on a nonprofit basis. After a slow start, the Packers finished the season with five straight wins to go 7-2-1 in their first season under new leadership.

1924 - Lambeau signed Verne Lewellen, the Packers' first legitimate star from outside Wisconsin and the surrounding states. Lewellen leads the Packers to a 7-4-0 season that includes a six-game winning streak.

1925 - The Packers moved into new City Stadium built on the grounds of East High School along the East River. The initial grandstand seating capacity was 6,000 with additional space beyond the end zones for standing room only customers.

- September 27, after four years of futility against Chicago teams, the Packers finally beat the Bears, 14-10, in Green Bay, but they lost to the Cardinals and the Bears in Chicago later in the year. The Packers' final record was 8-5, but it was only good for ninth place in a league that was crowded with several small-town teams.

1926 - October 31, the Packers beat the Cardinals for the first time, but they could only manage two ties against the Bears in three tries. Final record was 7-3-3 for fifth place.

1927 - October 23, an estimated crowd of 11,000 jammed into City Stadium to see the Packers play the New York Yankees and their star Red Grange. "The Gallopin' Ghost" didn't play, and the Packers won, 13-0.

   - The Packers finished the season with a record of 7-2-1 that included a win and a tie with the Cardinals.

1928 - The Packers tied the Bears in their first meeting of the season, then beat them twice in Chicago.

   - November 18, the Packers played the first of four games in 15 days of an eastern road trip, and they defeated the New York Giants, 7-0. They lost the next two and tied the last before the returned to the Midwest to finish the season on an upbeat note with a 6-0 win over the Bears in the Windy City.

1929 - Packers added halfback Johnny "Blood" McNally, tackle Cal Hubbard, and guard Mike Michalske to the roster, and this trio of stars led the Packers to their first-ever NFL title with an outstanding record of 12-0-1, the only blemish being a scoreless tie with the Frankford Yellowjackets. Packers allowed a meager 22 points in 13 games, while they tallied a whopping 198 for an average score of better than 15 to less than two.

1930 - The Packers became only the second team to win the NFL title in successive years, topping the standings with a 10-3-1 mark.

1931 - The Packers grabbed the brass ring for the third straight year to become the first and only team to win three titles in a row, a feat that they would repeat in the 1960s. They post a 12-2 record.

   - November 15, the Chicago Cardinals broke Green Bay's

unbeaten streak at 22 games with 21-13 upset at Comiskey Park in Chicago.

1932 - Rules of the day deprived the Packers of a fourth straight NFL crown as they finished with a record of 10-3-1 to the Chicago Bears' mark of 7-1-6 and the Portsmouth Spartans' tally of 7-1-4. Ties didn't count, so the Bears and Spartans tied for first with a winning percentage of .875, while the Packers were credited with a percentage of .769. If ties had counted as half a win and half a loss as in later years, the Packers' percentage would have been .750, while the Bears would have been at .714. Portsmouth would have matched at the Packers with a level of .750, thus forcing them to play an extra game to determine the champion. As it was, the Bears and Spartans met in Chicago Stadium in mid-December for the title, and they played the game that changed NFL history forever.

1933 - The NFL split into two divisions, Eastern and Western, with the Packers being assigned to the Western with the Bears, Cardinals, and Spartans. The Bears won the division crown, then the NFL championship with an exciting win over the New York Giants.

- The Packers suffered their first losing season with a dismal mark of 5-7-1.

1934 - While watching the Packers play, a slightly inebriated fan fell from the stands at City Stadium and suffered injuries that required him to be hospitalized. He subsequently sued the Packers and won an award of $5,000. The Packers' insurance company went bankrupt at this time and was unable to pay off the debt, leaving the corporation holding the bag. The Packers also filed for protection under the bankruptcy laws, and the court appointed a friendly receiver who kept the corporation in business and the team on the playing field until the debt was paid in full.

- On the gridiron, the Packers bounced back with a winning

record of 7-6-0 that was good enough for third place in the division.

- The Portsmouth Spartans were purchased by a Detroit businessman who moved the team to the Motor City and renamed then the Lions on the same theory that George Halas named his team the Bears. "If baseball players are tigers, then football players must be lions."

1935 - Lambeau outsmarted other NFL coaches who were seeking the services of an end from Alabama, and he signed Don Hutson to a contract.

- September 22, Hutson caught his first touchdown pass from Arnie Herber, and the Packers down the Bears, 7-0.

- Three losses to the Chicago Cardinals coupled with one to the Lions gave the Packers a mark of 8-4 for the year as they finished second in the division to eventual NFL champ Detroit.

1936 - The NFL began its Draft of college players, and the first player taken was Jay Berwanger from the University of Chicago. Ironically, Berwanger never played in the NFL. The Packers made Russ Letlow, a guard from the University of San Francisco, their first choice. Letlow turned out to be an outstanding professional player.

- The Packers were nearly perfect again as they suffered only a loss to the Bears and a tie with Cardinals on their way to a division title.

- December 13, the Packers faced the Boston Redskins for the NFL title. The game was played in New York because the owner of the Redskins, George Marshall, was angry with Boston fans for their lack of support for his team. The Packers handled the Redskins easily, winning 21-6 at the Polo Grounds.

1937 - The Packers lost their first two games of the season and their last two games to finish in a tie for second place in the division.

1938 - Lambeau drafted Cecil Isbell from Purdue, and the rookie passer led the Packers to the division crown with a mark of 8-3.

- December 11, the Packers squared off with the Giants at the Polo Grounds in New York and lost a close championship contest, 23-17.

1939 - The Packers won the Western Division title for the third time in four years, finishing strong with four straight wins on the road to go 9-2 for the year.

- December 10, in a rematch with the Giants for the NFL crown, the Packers crunched the New Yorkers, 27-0, in front of 32,279 fans in Milwaukee.

1940 - November 24, the Packers scored 50 points for the first time in a regular season NFL game as they crushed the Lions, 50-7, in Detroit. The huge victory wasn't enough to give them the division title and another shot at the NFL crown.

1941 - September 28, the Packers lost to the Bears in Green Bay for their only regular season defeat. They posted a record of 10-1, but so did the Bears.

- November 23, the Packers set a new record when they scored 54 points against the Steelers at Pittsburgh, winning, 54-7.

- December 14, a week after the Japanese bombed Pearl Harbor to start World War II for the United States the Packers and Bears faced each other in Chicago with the division title at stake. The Bears handled the Packers to the tune of 33-14.

1942 - November 1, the Packers mauled the Cardinals in Green

Bay, 55-24, to set another new scoring mark.

- Two losses to the Bears made the Packers bridesmaids again as they finished with a record of 8-2-1. The Packers also set a single season scoring mark when they tallied 300 points for the year.

1943 - The Bears won the Western Division crown for the fourth straight year, and the Packers finished second again.

1944 - The Packers started the season with six consecutive wins, including a 42-28 victory over the Bears on September 24 at City Stadium. They went on to wrest the Western Division title away from the Bears with a final record of 8-2.

- December 17, the Packers played the underdogs in the NFL championship game as they faced the Giants in New York. The Gothamites had pasted the Packers, 24-0, four weeks earlier on the same field, but on this day the upstart Packers from little Green Bay smacked the mighty men of the Big Apple, 14-7, to give Curly Lambeau his sixth and last NFL crown.

1945 - October 7, Don Hutson caught four TD passes and kicked five extra points in the second quarter of the game against the Lions in Milwaukee. This feat set the all-time record for points scored in a quarter by one player at 29. The Packers crushed Detroit, 57-21, to set another scoring record of their own.

- The Packers finished in third place in the division with a record of 6-4 as the Rams won the title in their last year in Cleveland.

1946 - Defense kept the Packers above .500 for the season as they finished in third place with a record of 6-5.

1947 - Lambeau went for more offense in the Draft, but the Packers suffered on defense as they once again finished in third place with a mediocre record of 6-5-1.

1948 - The glory was gone from City Stadium as the Packers could manage to win only three games and slip to fourth place in the division with a mark of 3-9, the worst record in Green Bay's history.

1949 - October 2, the Los Angeles Rams and their vaunted passing attack invaded City Stadium and humiliated the Packers, 48-7, in front of 24,308 fans. The loss was the Packers' ninth in a row, the longest losing streak in the team's history.

- With attendance falling dramatically for Milwaukee games, the Packers ran a poll for the fans to pick an all-time Packer team. The voters selected Arnie Herber at quarterback, Johnny Blood and Verne Lewellen as halfbacks, Clarke Hinkle at fullback, Don Hutson and Lavvie Dilweg as ends, Cal Hubbard and Cub Buck as tackles, Mike Michalske and Buckets Goldenberg as guards, and Charley Brock at center.

- November 25, Thanksgiving Day, to raise money for the failing franchise, the Packers played an intra-squad game and introduced the "All-Time" team. The event pulled in a neat $50,000, and the Packers remained afloat for the rest of the season.

- The Packers finished their worst season ever under Lambeau at 2-10.

1950 - After a long behind-the-scenes battle with corporation officials, Curly Lambeau, the so-called founder of the Packers, was forced to resign as head coach and vice-president. The next day he became the head coach and vice-president of the Chicago Cardinals.

- Gene Ronzani, a one-time Chicago Bear and graduate of Marquette, was hired to be the second head coach of the Packers, and he was elected vice-president of the corporation.

- A new stock drive netted $118,000, put the Packers on firm financial ground, and saved the team for the fans of Wisconsin and the Upper Peninsula of Michigan.

- Ronzani's first team was only one game better than Lambeau's last team, but optimism reigned supreme for the future of the team.

1951 - The Packers started strong with three wins in their first five games, but they weren't able to win another contest the rest of the year, losing seven straight to finish at 3-9 again.

1952 - September 28, the Bears extended the Packers' losing streak to eight games in front of a sellout crowd at City Stadium.

- October 5, with only 9,657 fans in the stands in Milwaukee, the Packers halted their losing ways with a 35-20 win over the Redskins. Green Bay went on to win five of their next seven before finishing dismally with three straight losses and winding up at 6-6 for the year.

1953 - November 26, Gene Ronzani was fired with two games remaining on the schedule because of a clause in his contract. If he had been allowed to stay for the final two contests on the West Coast, the corporation would have had to pay him for the next year. The Packers finished with a miserable 2-9-1 record.

1954 - Hoping to put some of the old college spirit back into the team, the Packers hired Lisle "Liz" Blackbourn, the head coach at Marquette to replace Ronzani. Blackbourn could only raise the team's record to 4-8 for the year.

1955 - September 25, the Packers opened the regular season with a major upset of the Detroit Lions, 20-17, at City Stadium.

- October 2, the Packers continued to roll with a sound win over the Bears, 24-3, at home.

- October 9, the hapless Baltimore Colts brought the Packers back to earth with 24-20 victory over Green Bay in Milwaukee.

- October 16, the Packers pulled off yet another upset by slipping past the Los Angeles Rams, 30-28, in Milwaukee.

- October 23, the Cleveland Browns crushed the Packers, 41-10, in a game that was never close. Reality set in with the Packers, and they went on to lose four more games and finish in third place with a mark of 6-6. Once again, the fans were optimistic about the future.

1956 - The voters of Green Bay approved a bond issue to build a new stadium for the Packers on the city's west side. Ground was broken for the new playing site in October.

- On the playing field, the Packers took two steps backward to finish the year at 4-8.

1957 - September 29, new City Stadium was completed just in time for the season, and it was dedicated at half-time of the Packers' season-opening victory over the Bears, 21-17.

- After the Packers finish with a record of 3-9, Blackbourn was fired by Packer executive Fred Trowbridge during a long distance phone call to the coach in Alabama. The executive committee adhered to the wishes of the fans and handed the coaching reins to longtime assistant coach Ray "Scooter" McLean.

1958 - April 28, Dominic Olejniczak, former mayor of Green Bay, was elected seventh president of the corporation. He would serve longer than any other person in that position.

- Discipline was nonexistent on the Green Bay roster as McLean proved Leo Durocher right when he said: "Nice guys finish last." The Packers suffered their worst season ever, 1-10-1, and McLean did the right thing by resigning at season's end.

1959 - February 4, after a long search, the Packers sign a new coach. His name was Vince Lombardi, an assistant with the New York Giants.

- September 27, the Packers squeaked by the Bears, 9-6, to start the Lombardi era in Green Bay on a positive note.

- November 15, the Packers lost their fifth in a row, and the fans were sure that nothing had changed in Green Bay with the coming of Lombardi.

- December 13, the Packers won their fourth straight to wrap up a 7-5 season, the first winning record for Green Bay in 12 years. The fans looked to the next year with guarded optimism.

1960 - September 25, the Bears eked out a 17-14 win over the Packers at City Stadium to open the season, and the fans were saying, "Here we go again."

- October 30, the Packers defeat the Steelers, 19-13, in Pittsburgh, for their fourth consecutive win.

- November 24, Thanksgiving Day, the Packers lost to the Lions on national television, 23-10, for their third defeat in the last four games. With their record at 5-4, the chances of a division title appeared dim.

- December 17, the Packers thumped the Rams, 35-21, in Los Angeles to win the Western Division title for the first time in 16 years. Paul Hornung finished the year with a record 176 points.

- December 26, the Packers met the Eagles in Philadelphia for the NFL championship and came up short, 17-13.

1961 - September 17, the Packers lost a tight one to the Lions, 17-13, at City Stadium, to open the season. Green Bay would then reel off six very convincing wins over San Francisco, the Bears, Baltimore, Cleveland, and two over the expansion Minnesota Vikings by a combined score of 209-51. The closest game was the second Viking contest, 28-10.

- November 5, the Colts ended the Packers' winning streak with a sound 45-21 victory at Baltimore.

- December 10, the Packers lost a tough one to the 49ers, 22-21, at San Francisco, for only their third loss of the year.

- December 17, the Packers butted the Rams, 24-17, at Los Angeles, to finish the regular season at 11-3 as they won the division title for the second year in a row. The Packers scored a record 415 points on the year for an average of 29.64 points per game, the highest average in their history.

- December 31, the Giants invaded Green Bay to meet the Packers for the NFL championship. The boys from the Big Apple were hardly up to it as the Packers gave them a sound drubbing, 37-0, to win their first NFL crown since 1944 and their seventh overall.

1962 - September 16, the Packers opened the defense of their crown with a 34-7 tromping of the Vikings at Green Bay.

- September 30, the Packers registered back-to-back shutouts for the first time since 1934 as they crushed the Bears, 49-0, at City Stadium. The previous week they slapped the Cardinals, 17-0, in Milwaukee. The win over the Bears was the largest margin of victory ever by the Packers in their long series with the "Monsters of the Midway".

- November 18, the Packers slip by the Colts, 17-13, in Green Bay to extend their winning streak to 10 games.

- November 22, Thanksgiving Day, once again the Packers were embarrassed by the Lions on national television, 26-14, and their winning streak was halted.

- December 16, the Packers finished the season with a 20-17 win over the Rams in Los Angeles. Green Bay's record was an outstanding 13-1, the second best in their long history.

- December 30, the Packers invaded New York to face the determined Giants once again for the NFL championship. Although not the blowout of the year before, the Packers handled the Giants with relative ease, 16-7, to keep the title in Green Bay.

1963 - Paul Hornung was suspended for a year for gambling.

- Without Hornung, the Packers lost twice to the Bears for their only defeats of the year, and they suffered a tie with the Lions on Thanksgiving Day to finish the year at 11-2-1 in second place behind the Bears who would win the NFL title against the Giants.

1964 - January 5, the Packers clipped the Cleveland Browns, 40-23, in the Playoff Bowl, a game for the second place teams in the two divisions of the league. Lombardi called it the "Losers Bowl".

- Packers lost two games by one point, a third by a field goal, and the season's finale ended in a tie as Green Bay suffered its worst season since Lombardi's inaugural year.

1965 - June 1, Earl L. "Curly" Lambeau, legendary founder of the Packers and first true head coach, died at age 67.

- December 26, after finishing in a regular season tie for first place in the Western Conference with Baltimore, the Packers played their first ever overtime game and defeated the Colts in sudden death, 13-10, in Green Bay on 25-yard field goal by Don Chandler.

1966 - January 2, the Packers started off the New Year on the right foot by winning their ninth NFL title with a sound victory over the Cleveland Browns, 23-12, in Green Bay.

- December 18, the Packers completed the regular season with a 12-2 record and another Western Conference crown, the only blemishes on the year coming in a one-point loss to San Francisco and a three-point setback to the Minnesota Vikings.

1967 - January 1, the Packers traveled to Dallas to face the Cowboys for the NFL title. A game-ending interception in the end zone by Packer Tom Brown allowed Green Bay to hold on for a 34-27 win and a chance to represent the NFL in the first ever Super Bowl.

- January 15, the Packers defeated the Kansas City Chiefs of the AFL, 35-10, at Los Angeles in the first Super Bowl.

- December 17, the Packers lost their season finale to the Pittsburgh Steelers, 24-17, in Green Bay, but despite losing their last two games, they won the Central Division title with a mark of 9-4-1.

- December 23, the Packers handed the Rams a lump of coal for Christmas as Green Bay dumped LA, 28-7, in the first round of the NFL playoffs in Milwaukee.

- December 31, with temperatures at Lambeau Field well below zero, the Packers hosted the Cowboys for the NFL title. In the closing seconds of the game, Dallas led 17-14, when Bart Starr plunged over the goal line with the winning touchdown to give the Packers the victory in the game that has come to be known as the "Ice Bowl".

1968 - January 14, the Packers basked in the sunshine of Miami, Florida, as the met the Oakland Raiders in the second Super Bowl.

Green Bay once again proved that the NFL was the superior league by trouncing the Raiders, 33-14, in a game that saw the first ever $3-million gate in professional football history.

- With the completion of the season, Lombardi stepped down as head coach of the Packers but remained as general manager. He promoted defensive assistant Phil Bengtson to be his replacement on the field.

- December 7, the Packers lost to the Colts, 16-3, in Green Bay, guaranteeing them their first losing season in 10 years.

- December 15, the Packers deprived the hated Bears of winning the Central Division title by nipping Chicago, 28-27, thus allowing the Minnesota Vikings to win their first ever division crown.

1969 - Unaware that he was suffering from colon cancer, Lombardi resigned as the Packers' general manager and became part-owner, executive vice-president, and head coach of the Washington Redskins. The Packer executive committee handed the GM post over to Bengtson.

- December 21, the Packers clobbered the St. Louis Cardinals, 45-28, in Green Bay, to close out a winning season with an 8-6 record, which was only good enough for third place in the four-team Central Division.

1970 - September 3, after a long hard bout with cancer, Vince Lombardi succumbed to the dreaded disease and took his place in the pantheon of football immortals.

- September 20, the sadness over the death of Lombardi carried into the first game of the season as the Packers were trounced by the Lions, 40-0; the worst defeat at Lambeau Field in Packer history.

- December 19, the Packers ended the season just like they started it. The Lions denied Green Bay a .500 season with a 20-0 shutout in the Motor City. The Packers closed out the year with six losses in their last eight games to finish at 6-8.

- December 21, Phil Bengtson resigned as head coach and general manager of the Packers. His record was 20-21-1 over three seasons for fourth place in Packer history (to date).

1971 - The executive committee hired Dan Devine away from the University of Missouri to be the Packers' next head coach and general manager.

- December 19, with nearly all of the stars of '60s now gone, the Packers finished their first season under Devine with a 27-6 loss in their first-ever meeting with the Miami Dolphins. The defeat at Miami was the first suffered by the Packers to a member of the former American Football League. The Packers had previously beaten the San Diego Chargers, Denver Broncos, and Cincinnati Bengals. Green Bay's record was a dismal 4-8-2.

1972 - September 17, the Packers started the season on the right foot by downing the Browns, 26-10, in Cleveland.

- October 8, Devine extended his winning string against the Bears to three straight with a 20-17 victory in Green Bay.
- November 12, Devine made it four in a row over the Bears with a 23-17 win in Chicago. Green Bay's record stood at 6-3.
- December 17, the Packers closed out the regular season with a 30-20 win over the Saints at New Orleans to win the NFC Central Division title with a record of 10-4.

- December 24, the Packers faced the Redskins in Washington in the first round of the NFL Playoffs and lost, 16-3. It was the last time the Packers would make the Playoffs for another decade.

1973 - November 4, the Packers lost to the Bears, 31-17, for the first time under Devine.

 - December 16, the Packers closed out a less than mediocre season with a win over the Bears, 21-0, in Green Bay.

1974 - Devine traded Green Bay's first, second, and third round Draft picks in 1975, and their first and second picks in '76 to the Los Angeles Rams for quarterback John Hadl. Prior to this transaction, Devine had traded away choices two, four, and five in 1973; and choices two, three, and four in 1974. The loss of all these Draft picks in such a short time proved detrimental to Green Bay's rebuilding plan and left the Packers buried deep in the lower tier of NFL teams for several years to come.

 - December 15, the Packers finished the season with a 10-3 loss to the Atlanta Falcons, their third straight defeat, all on the road. Their final record was 6-8.

 - December 19, the executive committee bought Dan Devine out of the final year of his contract before they learned that he had already signed a new contract to become the head coach at Notre Dame.

 - December 24, the executive committee gave Packer fans the Christmas gift of their wishes and dreams when they hired Bart Starr to be the Packers seventh official head coach and general manager.

1975 - September 21, the Packers began Starr's tenure at the helm with a 30-16 loss to the Lions in Milwaukee.

 - October 19, after four losses, Starr won his first game as a head coach with a 19-17 squeaker over the Dallas Cowboys in Dallas.

- November 16, the Packers lost their fourth in a row when the Lions beat them, 13-10, in Detroit.

- November 30, Starr beat the Bears for the first time, 28-7, and the Packers had their first winning streak—two games long—under Starr.

- December 21, the Packers finished the season on an upbeat note with a 22-13 win over the Falcons in Green Bay. Starr's first year record was 4-10.

1976 - Starr obtained quarterback Lynn Dickey in a trade with the Houston Oilers.

- September 26, the Packers lost to the Bengals, 28-7, in Cincinnati, for their third straight loss to open the season.

- October 17, the Packers beat the Eagles, 28-13, to even their record at 3-3.

- November 28, the Packers lost to the Bears for the second time in three weeks, guaranteeing them a losing season.

1977 - October 23, the Packers shut out the expansion Tampa Bay Buccaneers, 13-0, to snap a four-game losing streak.

- December 4, the Packers nipped the Lions, 10-9, in Green Bay, to end a five-game losing streak.

- December 18, the Packers beat the San Francisco 49ers, 16-14, in Milwaukee to end the season on a positive note. Starr's record in his third season was 4-10.

1978 - Starr picked wide receiver James Lofton from Stanford as the Packers first pick in the NFL Draft. With the second first round pick, Starr took linebacker John Anderson, a Wisconsin native who went to the University of Michigan. These two players would become the foundation for rebuilding the Packers into a competitive team in the '80s.

- September 3, the Packers opened in Detroit with a win over the Lions, 13-7.

- September 10, the Packers met the Saints in Milwaukee and came away with a 28-17 win. This was the first time since 1969 that the Packers started the season with two consecutive wins.

- September 24, after a loss to the Oakland Raiders in Green Bay, the Packers traveled to San Diego where they beat the Chargers, 24-3, to begin a four-game winning streak, their longest ever under Starr and the first since 1967.

- October 29, the Packers beat the Bucs, 9-7, on three Chester Marcol field goals as they reached their peak for the year at 7-2.

- November 26, the Packers played their first-ever regular season overtime game. After 75 minutes of play with the Vikings, the score remained tied at 10-all.

- December 17, the Packers missed the Playoffs by losing their last two games of the year, 14-0 to the Bears and 31-14 to the Rams; but they did have a winning season at 8-7-1, one of two under Starr.

1979 - September 2, with hopes up for a return to the glory of the Lombardi years, the Packers opened the season against the Bears in Chicago and were narrowly defeated in defensive contest, 6-3.

- September 16, the Packers lost to the eventual division winning Tampa Bay Bucs, 21-10, in Green Bay.

- September 23, the Packers and Vikings played their second straight overtime game, but this time Minnesota prevailed, 27-21.

- December 9, the Packers lost to the Bears, 15-14, in Green Bay. It was their fourth straight loss and 11th of the year. Only a win over the Lions in the last week kept Starr from suffering through his third 4-10 season in five years.

1980 - September 7, the Packers opened the season against the Bears in Green Bay. At the end of regulation, the game was tied, 6-6. In overtime, the Packers lined up to kick a game-winning field goal, but the Bears blocked Chester Marcol's kick—right back into Marcol's unexpecting hands. Running for his life, Marcol skirted around the left side and made it into the end zone to give the Packers a 12-6 victory.

- October 5, the Packers slipped by the Bengals, 14-9, in Green Bay to end a three-game losing streak.

- December 7, with only three games left in the season, the Packers must win every game to have a winning season. The Bears put a stop to that notion by handing the Packers their worst defeat ever, 61-7, in Chicago. The Packers went on to be humiliated twice more that year and wound up with a record of 5-10-1.

1981 - September 6, the Packers achieved a small measure of revenge on the Bears by beating them, 16-9, in the season opener at Chicago.

- October 4, the Packers halted a three-game losing streak with a win over the New York Giants, 27-14.

- November 1, after going 2-6 in the first half of the season, the Packers started the second half with a 34-24 win over the Seattle Seahawks.

- November 15, for the first time in Starr's tenure as head coach, the Packers swept the Bears with a 21-17 win in Green Bay.

- December 20, the Packers faced a do-or-die situation against the New York Jets. A win would have put them in the Playoffs for the first time under Starr, but the Jets dashed their hopes by soundly defeating the Pack, 28-3.

1982 - May 3, Judge Robert J. Parins was elected president of the Green Bay Packers, Inc., succeeding Dominic Olejniczak. Parins was the first full-time chief executive in the club's history.

- Packers built a 55,000-square foot indoor practice facility.

- Ron Hallstrom, a guard from Iowa, was the Packers first pick in the NFL Draft.

- After two weeks of play, the NFL Players Union went on strike, halting the season for two months. The Packers opened with wins over the Rams, 35-23, in Milwaukee, and the Giants, 27-19, at the Meadowlands on Monday Night Football. When play resumed in November, the Packers beat the Vikings, 26-7, in Milwaukee to give them their first 3-0 record to start a season since 1966. Lost during the strike were both games with the Bears, ending the longest playing streak between to NFL teams to date.

- December 26, the Packers crushed the Falcons, 38-7, in Atlanta, to win the division title, which was meaningless that year because of the strike. The win did gain a Playoff berth for the Packers as the NFL decided to hold a tournament between the eight teams in each conference with the best records. The Packers finished fourth in the NFC.

1983 - January 8, the Packers hosted a Playoff game at Lambeau Field for the first since 1967 when they defeated the Cowboys in the now legendary "Ice Bowl". Lynn Dickey, James Lofton, and John Jefferson led the Packers to resounding 41-16 win over the St. Louis Cardinals.

- January 16, the Packers lost their second round game to the Cowboys, 37-26, at Dallas.

- September 4, after building a lead of 35-0 in the first half, the Packers had to go to overtime to defeat the Houston Oilers, 41-38, in the season opener.

- October 2, the Packers crushed the Bucs, 55-14, to up their record to 3-2 on the season.

- October 17, in the most exciting and highest scoring game in Monday Night Football history, the Packers narrowly avoided a defeat at the hands of the Redskins when the Washington place-kicker missed a last minute field goal from mid-range. Final score: 48-47.

- December 18, the Bears denied the Packers a shot at the Playoffs by defeating them, 23-21, in Chicago. The Packers finished the season at 8-8.

- December 19, after nine years as head coach of the Packers, Bart Starr was fired as head coach. Starr's record as head coach was 53-77-3.

- December 24, the executive committee hired former Packer Forrest Gregg to be head coach of the Packers for the next five years.

1984 - September 2, the Packers opened the season with a close win over the St. Cardinals, 24-23, to start Gregg's tenure on the right foot.

- October 21, the Packers lost their seventh game in a row when they went down to defeat to the Seattle Seahawks, 30-24, at Milwaukee.

- October 28, the Packers began a second-half turnaround with a

41-9 shellacking of the Lions in Green Bay.

- December 16, the Packers concluded a sound comeback in the second half by whipping the Vikings, 30-14, in Minnesota. Green Bay finished the season at 8-8, and fans looked forward to the next year.

1985 - The Packers built 72 private luxury boxes at Lambeau Field to increase seating capacity to 56,926.

- The Packers picked tackle Ken Ruettgers from Southern California in the first round of the NFL Draft.

- September 8, hoping to pick up where they left off the year before, the Packers opened the season against the Patriots and lost a close one, 26-20.

- October 12, John B. Torinus, Sr., Packer board member for 37 years, corporation secretary, and member of the executive committee for 35 years, died at his summer home in Door County. He was 72.

- After going 3-5 in the first half, the Packers went 5-3 in the second half of the season to finish at .500 for the second year in a row under Gregg.

1986 - The Packers reported their first $2 million profit in their history.

- October 19, the Packers nipped the Browns, 17-14, in Cleveland to end their six-game losing streak, their longest ever at the beginning of a season.

- December 20, the New York Giants, eventual Super Bowl champions, pounded the Packers, 55-24, to close out the season. The Packers finished fourth in the division with a record of 4-12.

1987 - May 6, the Green Bay Packer Foundation, a vehicle to assure the continued contributions to charity, was established.

- The Packers reported their first $3 million dollar profit in their history.

- Quarterback Randy Wright held out for more money, giving 10th round draft choice Don Majkowski a chance to show his stuff to the coaching staff. Majkowski is able to stick with the team, and after the 1988 season, Wright is history.

- The NFL players union went on strike after two games, but the owners countered by hiring replacement players and continuing the schedule. After three weeks of replacement games, the union caved in and the regulars returned to play.

- The Packers played three overtime games in the first five contests of the season, winning one, losing one, and tying one. After six weeks, their record was 3-2-1, and hopes were high that a Playoff spot was in the offing. It wasn't to be as the Packers finished 5-9-1.

1988 - January 15, Forrest Gregg surprised everybody by resigning from the Packers in order to return to his college alma mater, Southern Methodist University, to rebuild its sagging football program as head coach and athletic director.

- February 3, the Packers hired Lindy Infante, offensive co-ordinator for the Cleveland Browns, to replace Gregg as head coach.

- October 9, in an attempt to rebuild the Packers in his image of pro football, Infante suffered through a five-game losing streak before winning his first game as an NFL head coach. The Packers trounced the New England Patriots, 45-3.

- December 11, the Packers broke a seven-game losing streak by dumping the Vikings, 18-6, in Green Bay.

- December 18, the Packers ended the season on a positive note by beating the Phoenix Cardinals, 26-17, in Arizona.

1989 - June 5, Judge Robert J. Parins retired as president of the Packers, but was elected chairman of the board of directors. Robert E. Harlan was elected to replace Parins as president and chief executive officer.

- August 22, the Packers announced plans for construction of 1,920 club seats in the south end zone of Lambeau Field and 36 additional private boxes.

- September 10, the Packers lose a heartbreaker to Tampa Bay, 23-21, in Green Bay.

- September 17, the excitement was back at Lambeau Field as the Packers came from behind to beat the Saints, 35-34.

- September 24, in a real barnburner, the Packers lost another close one, this time to the Rams, 41-39, in LA.

- October 1, for the fourth straight week, the outcome of the game was in doubt until the final seconds as the Packers nipped the Falcons, 23-21, in Milwaukee.

- October 8, the Packers beat the hapless Cowboys, 31-13, in Green Bay.

- October 22, the Packers lost another heartbreaker, this time to the Miami Dolphins, 23-20.

- November 5, the Packers defeated the Bears, 14-13, on a controversial call. The refs on the field called back a TD pass by

Majkowski, stating that he was over the line of scrimmage when he threw it, but the "Instant Replay" official reversed the call to allow the TD to stand.

- December 24, the Packers beat the Cowboys, 20-10, in Dallas to finish the season at 10-6 for their first winning campaign since 1982.

- December 25, the Packers' Playoff hopes were dashed when the Vikings won their season finale on Monday Night Football.

1990 - January 16, the executive committee extended Lindy Infante's contract through the 1994 season.

- Don Majkowski held out for more money and a guaranteed contract. After he signed and reported to camp, it was learned that he had a shoulder injury left over from the previous year. He missed the first few games of the season.

- September 9, the Packers opened the season with high hopes again, and reserve quarterback Anthony Dilweg led the team to a convincing 36-24 victory over the Rams in Green Bay.

- November 4, the Packers ended the first half of the season at 3-5 when they lost a close one to the 49ers, 24-20, in Green Bay.

- December 30, after starting the second half of the year with three straight wins, the Packers lost their last five games, including a 22-13 defeat at the hands of the Denver Broncos to end the year.

1991 - January 7, the Packers hired Michael R. Reinfeldt, former Pro Bowl safety and Oakland Raiders executive, to be the chief financial officer for the corporation.

- The names of 18 Packer players and coaches elected to the Pro Football Hall of Fame were placed in permanent display on the green walls between floors of Lambeau Field's private boxes on both sides of the stadium, with the team's 11 NFL championship years emblazoned above the club seats in the south end zone.

- November 20, executive vice-president of football operations Tom Braatz, was relieved of his duties while he was out of town. He learned of the change when he arrived at Austin Straubel Field and was informed of it by the media.

- November 27, the executive committee hired Ron Wolf, director of player personnel for the New York Jets and a veteran of 29 years as a pro football scout and executive. As executive vice-president and general manager, Wolf was given full authority to run the Packers' football operations.

- December 21, the Packers closed out a poor season with a meaningless victory over the Vikings, 27-7.

- December 22, the win over the Vikings failed to help Lindy Infante keep his job. Wolf fired him.

1992 - January 11, Wolf hired San Francisco offensive co-ordinator Mike Holmgren to be the Packers 11th head coach.

- February, Wolf traded a first round draft choice to the Atlanta Falcons for backup quarterback Brett Favre.

- In his first NFL Draft with the Packers, Wolf selected wide receiver Robert Brooks, running back Edgar Bennett, quarterback Ty Detmer, and tight end Mark Chmura.

- September 6, the Holmgren era began with an exciting overtime loss to the Vikings, 23-20, in Green Bay. Despite the loss, Packer fans were encouraged by their team's play.

- September 20, Don Majkowski went down with a first quarter injury, and reserve Brett Favre came off the bench to lead the Packers to a come-from-behind victory over the Bengals, 24-23. Favre hit wide receiver Kitrick Taylor with a 35-yard scoring strike with 13 seconds left on the clock.

- September 27, Favre started his first game for the Packers and led Green Bay to a 17-3 win over the Steelers.

- November 15, the Packers beat the Eagles, 27-24, in Milwaukee to begin a six-game winning streak.

- December 27, the Packers were once again a win away from the Playoffs when they faced the Vikings in Minnesota. They came up short, 27-7. The Packers finished with a 9-7 record to make Holmgren only the third coach in Packer history to be a winner in his first season at the helm.

1993 - April 9, the Packers signed free agent defensive end Reggie White, the most sought after unrestricted player on the market.

- July, the new 25,000-square foot edition to the Packers' training quarters, housing an 84-by-70 foot gymnasium and new public relations and marketing offices, was completed.

- September 5, the Packers opened the season in Milwaukee with a convincing win over the Rams, 36-6.

- October 3, after two narrow losses, the Packers were trounced by the Cowboys, 36-14, in Dallas.

- October 31, the Packers won their third straight by dumping the Bears, 17-3, at home.

- November 28, the Packers beat the Bucs, 13-10, in Green Bay to cap their second three-game winning streak of the season.

- December 26, the Packers crushed the Raiders, 28-0, in Green Bay to clinch a Playoff spot.

1994 - January 2, the Packers lose to the Lions, 30-20, at the Pontiac Silverdome, to tie for second place in the division. For the second straight year, the Packers finished with a record of 9-7.

- January 8, in a strange twist of events, the Packers had to travel to the Pontiac Silverdome for the second straight week to meet the Lions in the first round of the Playoffs, but this time they came out on top, 28-24, to advance to the second round

- January 16, the Packers faced the Cowboys in Dallas and were eliminated from the Playoffs, 27-17.

- March 31, the Packers extended the contract of Ron Wolf through the 1999 season.

- April 21, Bob Harlan announced plans to construct an additional 90 private boxes and a 57-seat auxiliary press box at Lambeau Field.

- July 18, the Don Hutson Center, the Packers' new indoor practice facility, was dedicated.

- August 25, the Packers extended the contract of head coach Mike Holmgren through the 1999 season.

- September 4, the Packers beat the Vikings, 16-10, for the first time under Holmgren.

- September 25, after losing to Miami and Philadelphia, the Packers beat the Bucs, 30-3, in Green Bay.
- October 12, the Packers announced that the team will no longer play any regular season or pre-season games in Milwaukee, beginning with the 1995 campaign.

- October 31, the Packers finished the first half of the season with a 33-6 shellacking of the Bears in Chicago during a driving rainstorm that made Soldiers Field a quagmire.

- November 13, the Packers capped a three-game winning streak by beating the New York Jets, 17-10, in Green Bay.

- December 11, the Bears came to Green Bay, and the Packers played rude hosts, tromping the visitors, 40-3, to break a three-game losing streak.

- December 24, the Packers traveled to Florida with hopes of making the Playoffs for the second year in a row, and they trimmed the Bucs, 34-19, to gain a playoff spot at home against the Lions. Wide receiver Sterling Sharpe aggravated an earlier neck injury and was forced to leave the game in the second half. For the third consecutive year, the Packers had a 9-7 record, but more important, it was their third straight winning season under Mike Holmgren.

- December 31, without Sterling Sharpe in the lineup, the Packers beat Lions in the first round of the Playoffs, 16-12. The victory was the Packers' 15th in post-season play over the years, and it kept them undefeated at home, 8-0, in Playoff competition.

1995 - February 28, the Packers released all-time career receptions leader Sterling Sharpe after he refused to accept a new contract that would pay him only $200,000 while he sat out the 1995 season recuperating from neck surgery.

- August, construction on additional private boxes was completed.

- September 3, the Packers opened the season at home against the St. Louis Rams amid predictions that Green Bay would finish no higher than third in the Central Division. Their 17-14 loss to the Rams did nothing to dispel this notion.

- September 11, the Packers helped the Bears worsen their record on Monday Night Football by handing them a 27-24 defeat in Chicago.

- September 24, the Packers beat the expansion Jacksonville Jaguars, 24-14, for their third win in a row.

- October 8, the Packers string of losses to the Dallas Cowboys was extended to six games when the Texans dumped the Pack, 34-24, in the Lone Star state.

- October 22, the Packers took it to the Vikings, 38-21, in Green Bay to run their record to 5-2 and keep pace with the Bears for the division lead.

- November 12, the Packers snapped a two-game losing skid by trimming the Bears, 35-28, in a game at Lambeau Field that featured more than a thousand all-purpose yards between the two teams.

- December 3, the Packers won their fourth straight and ninth of the season when they handled the Bengals with comparative ease at Lambeau, 24-10.

- December 16, the Packers traveled to the Crescent City to take on the Saints and hopefully to clinch a Playoff spot. Their wishes were granted as they stuck it to New Orleans, 34-23, in the Louisiana Superdome.

- December 24, the Pittsburgh Steelers came to Lambeau Field on Christmas Eve, and Pittsburgh's top wide receiver, Yancey Thigpen gave the Green Bay fans a great Christmas gift when he dropped a last minute, fourth down TD pass that allowed the Packers to win the NFC Central Division title in a non-strike year for the first time since 1972. The Packers finished the regular season with a record of 11-5, giving Mike Holmgren his fourth winning campaign in as many years.

- December 31, the Packers hosted the Atlanta Falcons in the first round of the Playoffs and clipped their wings, 37-20, to keep the home Playoff record intact at 9-0.

1996 - January 6, the Packers traveled to San Francisco to take on the defending Super Bowl champion 49ers. Oddsmakers had the Packers as underdogs, but the green-and-gold faithful smelled an upset all week long. The Packers missed an early scoring opportunity, but they made up for it later and dumped the 49ers, 27-17, to earn a shot at the Super Bowl the following week.

- January 14, once more the Packers had to square off against the Cowboys in Texas in the post-season, and for the third straight year, Dallas came out on top, this time, 38-27.

- Off-season, Packers signed free agents Desmond Howard (wr-kr), Don Beebe (wr-kr), and Ron Cox (lb).

- April, Packers used first-round NFL Draft pick to take offensive tackle John Michels from Southern California to replace aging veteran Ken Ruettgers.

- September 1, Packers opened season with mechanical victory over hapless Buccaneers at Tampa. Brett Favre threw four TD passes, three to tight end Keith Jackson; Chris Jacke booted two field goals; and defense smothered Bucs, intercepting four passes, two by Leroy Butler. Final score: 34-3 Packers.

- September 9, Packers hosted Philadelphia Eagles on Monday Night Football. Packers scored 23 points before Eagles get on the board in the second quarter. Favre threw three more TD passes, two to wide receiver Robert Brooks; and defense intercepted three more passes. Final score: 39-13 Packers.

- September 15, San Diego Chargers, losers to San Francisco in Super Bowl XXIX, came to Green Bay for a lesson in humility. Favre threw three more TD passes to give him 10 on the season so far. Edgar Bennett rushed for a six. Leroy Butler intercepted two more passes and returned one 90 yards for a score. Packers now have nine interceptions for the year. Kick return specialist Desmond Howard returned a punt 65 yards for the Packers final TD of the day. Final score: 42-10 Packers.

- September 22, Packers traveled to Minneapolis to face equally the undefeated Minnesota Vikings in the Metrodome. Green Bay took a 21-17 lead into the fourth quarter. After pinning the Vikes deep in their own territory with third and long, Packers defense rushed only the down linemen and put up an umbrella defense to guard against the long bomb. Viking QB Warren Moon found receiver Jake Reed under the coverage for a first down. Vikings marched down field to score go-ahead TD and eventually win, knocking Packers into second place. Favre threw two TD passes, and defense picked off two, one by linebacker George Koonce who returned it 75 yards for a six. Final score: 30-21 Vikings.

- September 29, Packers traveled to Seattle to meet shaky Seahawks in the Kingdome. Favre threw four more TD passes, two to second-year wide receiver Antonio Freeman. Favre now has 16 TD passes for the year. Defense picked off four more passes to raise their total to 15 for the season. Final score: 31-10 Packers.

- October 6, Packers breezed into the Windy City for game six. Bears put up brave fight for first quarter, then Favre found Brooks, Jackson, and Freeman for scores in the second period to put Packers up, 20-3, at the half. Bears stormed back in the third stanza with a field goal before kick returner-wide receiver Don Beebe returned the ensuing kickoff 90 yards for a touchdown. Favre connected with Freeman for another six, and Packers coasted home. Defense snared three Dave Krieg throws to raise their total on the year to 18, and Favre's TD pass sum is now 20. Final score: 37-6 Packers.

- October 14, the San Francisco 49ers came to Lambeau for a bout with the Packers on Monday Night Football. Frisco was without the services of starting quarterback Steve Young. Green Bay suffered a major blow on the very first play from scrimmage when Robert Brooks blew out his right knee making a cut in his pattern. The injury ended the season for Brooks and seriously jeopardized his career. Don Beebe filled in for Brooks, caught 11 passes for 220 yards and a TD. The Packers took the early lead, 6-0, on a pair of field goals by Chris Jacke, but the 49ers stormed back in the second quarter to score 17 points and take the half-time lead, 17-6. Favre and Beebe hooked up on a controversial TD in the third stanza. Replay showed clearly that the ball touched the ground, but game officials ruled it a catch. A 49er claimed to have touched Beebe while he was down around the 12, but Beebe bounced up without hesitation and raced into the end zone. Officials signaled touchdown, and the play stood up on the scoreboard. Favre then connected with Bennett for a 2-point conversion to bring the Packers within three. Jacke tied the game in the fourth quarter with his third field goal of the night. The Packers got the ball back with under two minutes to go. Rookie wide receiver Derrick Mayes ran the wrong pattern, and Favre was intercepted deep in Packer country. The 49ers settled for a field goal and appeared to have the game put away with less than a minute to go. Favre had other plans as he mastered a drive that put Jacke within range in the closing seconds. Jacke tied the game again, and it's overtime. The Packers mounted a drive that was stopped on the San Francisco 36. Coach Mike Holmgren made the risky call, and Jacke split the uprights from 53 yards out for his fifth field goal of the night, and the Packers celebrated another victory. Final score: 23-20 Packers.

- October 27, after a week off, the Packers hosted the rejuvenated Bucs from Tampa Bay. The Packers were without the services of both of their starting wide receivers as now Antonio Freeman is down with a broken leg. Favre and company appeared lethargic but managed to win. Final score: 13-7 Packers.

- November 3, the Lions came to Lambeau Field. Terry Mickens returned from an injury and snared two TD passes to spark the Packers in their eighth win of the year. Final score: 28-18 Packers.

- November 10, the Packers traveled to Kansas City. The Chiefs surprised Green Bay with an aggressive running attack. Although Favre had a good day, the Packers played catch-up all day and fell short. Tight end Mark Chmura injured an arch in his foot and missed most of the game. Final score: 27-20 Kansas City.

- November 18, the Packers were in Big D to take on the resurgent Cowboys. With Brooks, Freeman, and Chmura all out with injuries, the Green Bay passing attack was lacking in excitement. The defense was able to keep the Cowboys out of the end zone, but kicker Chris Boniol tied an NFL record by booting seven field goals in a game. Favre was unable to find new wide receiver Andre Rison, and the Cowboys pulled off yet another win over the Pack. Final score: 21-6 Dallas.

- November 24, the Packers played their third road game in as many weeks. The opponent was St. Louis in the new Trans World Dome. After a lethargic first half, the Packers came to life in the third quarter and dumped the Rams to end their brief losing streak at two games. Final score: 24-9 Packers.

- December 1, the Bears came to Green Bay. Chicago scored first, last, and in the middle for 17 points, but sandwiched neatly between the first Chicago TD and field goal were two TD's by the Packers and another pair of sixes between the field goal and the second Chicago TD. Desmond Howard broke a 75-yard punt return for six in the third quarter that electrified the crowd. Final score: 28-17 Packers.

- December 8, the Denver Broncos came to Lambeau in what many thought would be a preview of Super Bowl XXXI.

Unfortunately, the Broncos chose not to play starting quarterback John Elway, tainting the contest from the outset. Denver's offense never mounted any serious threats without Elway, but the Packer offense completely dominated the Broncos. Favre threw four TD passes, three going to Freeman. Final score: 41-6 Packers.

- December 15, with the Central Division crown in the trophy room already, the Packers met the Lions in the Pontiac Silverdome. The Lions barely went through the motions as head coach Wayne Fontes faced termination at the end of the season. Howard returned another punt for a TD, this one for 92 yards. Final score: 31-3 Pack.

- December 22, the Packers were playing for home field advantage throughout the Playoffs when the Vikings came to Lambeau Field. All they needed was a win or a tie. Minnesota put up a decent fight for the first half, but the Packers dominated them completely in the second half. Favre threw three more TD passes to give him 39 for the year, a new team record. Packers finished the year at 13-3. Final score: 38-10 Packers.

1997 - January 4, the Divisional Playoff round. The 49ers were the Packers' first obstacle on their road to New Orleans. San Francisco quarterback Steve Young made a game attempt at playing, but he had to leave after playing just two short series. In between, Desmond Howard electrified the crowd again with a punt return for 71 yards and the first score of the contest. The Packers scored twice more in the half before the 49ers put up seven points. San Francisco tried to make a game of it with a TD in the third quarter, but the Packers scored twice more to put it away. Final score: 35-14 Pack.

- January 12, the National Football Conference Championship was at stake when the astounding Carolina Panthers, a second-year expansion team, came to Lambeau for the very first meeting ever with the Packers. Carolina scored to take a first quarter lead, 7-0. The Packers tied it early in the second period on a 29-yard pass play from Favre to Dorsey Levens. Carolina added a field goal to go up,

10-7, but it was the last time the Panthers would lead in the game. Favre found Freeman with a six-yard touchdown, and Jacke kicked a 31-yard field goal with 10 seconds left in the half to give Green Bay a 17-10 lead. The two teams exchanged field goals before Bennett crossed the goal line from four yards out to put the Packers up, 27-13. The Green Bay defense held the Carolina offense at arm's length for the remainder of the game, and Jacke put up one more field goal. Final score: 30-13 Packers.

- January 26, Super Bowl XXXI in New Orleans. After an absence 29 years, the Packers returned to the NFL championship game to play for the title and the trophy that bears the name of the legendary Vincent T. Lombardi. Opposing the Packers were the New England Patriots. The Packers were heavy favorites to extend the NFC's Super Bowl winning streak to 13, while the Patriots were poised to upset Green Bay.

The Packers started strong, with Favre throwing a 54-yard bomb to Andre Rison in the first quarter. This was followed by a Chris Jacke field goal from 37 yards. The Patriots struck back quickly with two first period TDs to take a 14-10 lead into the second quarter. The Packers owned the second stanza, scoring 17 points on a record-setting scoring toss from Favre to Antonio Freeman for 81 yards, a Jacke field goal from 31 yards, and a TD sprint by Favre around end for two yards. New England came back strong in the third period to make the game close at 27-21, but Desmond Howard and the kickoff return team stemmed the tide by taking the ensuing kickoff back 99 yards to put the game into the hands of the Green Bay defense. The two offenses seemed fairly even, but the Packer defenders proved to be the difference in the outcome. Brian Williams, Mike Prior, Doug Evans, and Craig Newsome each intercepted a pass, and Reggie White, the "Minister of Defense", set a Super Bowl record with three sacks. The Favre to Freeman TD pass set another Super Bowl record for longest play from scrimmage, and Howard set three records: Longest Kickoff Return; Longest Kickoff Return Average, Career (minimum 4), 35.4; and Most Punt Return Yards, Game, 90. Six individual records were tied. Five team records were set by the two teams, and eight team records were tied. Final score: 35-21 Packers.

- April 19, Packers drafted Ross Verba, an offensive tackle from Iowa, in the first round of the NFL College Draft.

- July 25, the Packers made Brett Favre the highest paid player in the NFL with a five-year contract extension that will keep him in Green Bay through the year 2002.

CRAIG HENTRICH

INDIVIDUAL RECORDS

RUSHING
Attempts

Most Attempts (career)

1,811, Jim Taylor, 1958-1966, gained 8,207 yards, averaged 4.53 per carry and 201 carries per season.

1,293, John Brockington, 1971-77, gained 5,024 yards, averaged 3.89 yards per carry and 185 carries per season.

1,171, Clarke Hinkle, 1932-41, gained 3,860 yards, averaged 3.30 yards per carry and 117 carries per season.

1,025, Tony Canadeo, 1941-44 and 1946-52, gained 4,197 yards, averaged 4.09 yards per carry and 93 carries per season.

Most Attempts (season)

284, Terdell Middleton, 1978 (16 games), for 1,116 yards, average 3.9 yards per carry.

274, John Brockington, 1972 (14 games), for 1,027 yards, average 3.7 yards per carry.

272, Jim Taylor, 1962 (14 games), for 1,474 yards, averaged 5.4 yards per carry.

Most Attempts (game)

39, Terdell Middleton, vs. Minnesota, Nov. 26, 1978 (110 yards), 2.82 yards per carry.

32, Jim Grabowski, vs. Chicago Bears, Sept. 24, 1967, 111 yards, 3.47 yards per carry.

32, John Brockington, at Minnesota , Nov. 17, 1974, 137 yards, 4.28 yards per carry.

30, Jim Taylor, vs. Pittsburgh, Nov. 3, 1963, 141 yards, 4.70 per carry.

30, John Brockington, at Chicago Bears, Nov. 7, 1971, 142 yards, 4.73 yards per carry.

30, Harlan Huckleby, at New York Giants, Oct. 4, 1981, 88 yards, 2.93 yards per carry.

29, Edgar Bennett, at Chicago Bears, Nov. 22, 1992, 107 yards, 3.69 yards per carry.

Most Attempts, Rookie (season)

216, John Brockington, 1971.

126, Gerry Ellis, 1980.

121, Willard Harrell, 1975.

114, Kenneth Davis, 1986.

108, Bob Monnett, 1933.

Yardage

Most Yards Gained (career)

8,207, Jim Taylor, 11seasons, 1,811 attempts, averaged 4.53 yards per carry and 746 yards per season.

5,024, John Brockington, 7 seasons, 1,293 attempts, averaged 3.89 yards per carry and 718 yards per season.

4,197, Tony Canadeo, 11 seasons, 1,025 attempts, averaged 4.09 yards per carry and 382 yards per season.

3,860, Clarke Hinkle, 10 seasons, 1,171 attempts, averaged 3.30 yards per carry and 386 yards per season .

3,826, Gerry Ellis, 7 seasons, 836 attempts, averaged 4.57 yards per carry and 547 yards per season.

3,711, Paul Hornung, 9 seasons, 893 attempts, averaged 4.16 yards per carry and 412 yards per season.

3,353, Edgar Bennett, 5 seasons, 936 attempts, 3.6 yards per carry and

671 yards per season.

Most Yards Gained (season)
1,474, Jim Taylor, 1962, 272 attempts.
1,307, Jim Taylor, 1961, 243 attempts.
1,169, Jim Taylor, 1964, 235 attempts.
1,144, John Brockington, 1973, 265 attempts.
1,116, Terdell Middleton, 1978, 284 attempts.
1,105, John Brockington, 1971, 216 attempts.
1,101, Jim Taylor, 1960, 230 attempts.
1,067, Edgar Bennett, 1995, 312 attempts.
1,052, Tony Canadeo, 1949, 208 attempts.
1,027, John Brockington, 1972, 274 attempts.
1,018, Jim Taylor, 1963, 248 attempts.

Most Yards Gained (game)
186, Jim Taylor, vs. New York Giants, Dec. 3, 1961, 27 attempts.
167, Billy Grimes, vs. New York Yanks, Oct. 8, 1950, 10 attempts.
165, Jim Taylor, at Los Angeles Rams, Dec.13, 1964, 17 attempts.
164, Jim Taylor, at Minnesota, Oct. 14, 1962, 17 attempts.

Longest Run From Scrimmage
97 yards, Andy Uram, vs. Chicago Cardinals, Oct. 8, 1939.
84 yards, Jim Taylor, vs. Detroit, Nov. 8, 1964.
83 yards, James Lofton, at New York Giants, Sept. 20, 1982.
80 yards, Jessie Clark, at St. Louis Cardinals, Sept. 29, 1985.
77 yards, Tom Moore, vs. Detroit, Sept. 22, 1963.
76 yards, Terdell Middleton, vs. Detroit, Oct. 1, 1978.
73 yards, Billy Grimes, at Chicago Bears, Oct. 15, 1950.

Most Games, 100 or More Yards Rushing (career)
26, Jim Taylor.
13, John Brockington.
9, Tony Canadeo.
6, Edgar Bennett
5, Terdell Middleton.
5, Eddie Lee Ivery.
5, Gerry Ellis.

Most Seasons, 1,000 or more Yards Rushing
5, Jim Taylor, 1960-64.
3, John Brockington, 1971-73.
1, Tony Canadeo, 1949.
1, Terdell Middleton, 1978.
1, Edgar Bennett, 1995.

Most Yards Gained, Rookie (season)
1,105, John Brockington, 1971.
545, Gerry Ellis, 1980.
519, Kenneth Davis, 1986.
445, Cecil Isbell, 1938.
412, Bobby Monnett, 1933.
394, Floyd Reid, 1950.
379, Walt Schlinkman, 1946.
365, Dave Hampton, 1969.
359, Willard Harrell, 1975.

Most Games, 100 or More Yards Rushing (season)
7, Jim Taylor, 1962.
5, Tony Canadeo, 1949.
5, Jim Taylor, 1960.
4, Jim Taylor, 1961, 1963-64.
4 John Brockington, 1971, 1973.
4, Terdell Middleton, 1978.

Most Consecutive Games, 100 or More Yards Rushing
3, John Brockington, 1971
2, Tony Canadeo, 1949 (twice).
2, Tobin Rote, 1951.
2, Jim Taylor, 8 times.
2, John Brockington, 1973.

Most Touchdowns (season)
19, Jim Taylor, 1962
15, Jim Taylor, 1961.

Most Touchdowns, Rookie (season)
5, Buckets Goldenberg, 1933; Gerry Ellis, 1980; Brent Fullwood, 1987.
4, Bobby Monnett, 1933.
4, Charlie Sample, 1942.
4, Tom Moore, 1960.
4, Dave Hampton, 1969.
4, John Brockington, 1971.
4, Scott Hunter, 1971.

FORWARD PASSING
Passes
Most Passes Completed (career)
1,808, Bart Starr, 1956-71, 16 seasons.
1,667, Brett Favre, 5 seasons.
1,592, Lynn Dickey, 9 seasons.
889, Don Majkowski, 6 seasons.
826, Tobin Rote, 7 seasons.
602, Randy Wright, 5 seasons.

Most Passes Completed (season)
363, Brett Favre, 1994, 582 attempts.
359, Brett Favre, 1995, 570 attempts.
353, Don Majkowski, 1989, 599 attempts.
325, Brett Favre, 1996, 543 attempts.
318, Brett Favre, 1993, 572 attempts.
302, Brett Favre, 1992, 471attempts.
289, Lynn Dickey, 1983, 484 attempts.
278, Lynn Dickey, 1980, 478 attempts.

Most Passes Completed (game)
36, Brett Favre, at Chicago Bears, Dec. 5, 1993, 54 attempts.
35, Lynn Dickey, at Tampa Bay, Oct. 12, 1980, 51 attempts.
34, Don Majkowski, at Detroit, Nov. 12, 1989, 59 attempts.
33, Brett Favre, at Atlanta, Oct. 4, 1992, 43 attempts.
31, Brett Favre, vs. Cincinnati, Dec. 3, 1995, 43 attempts & vs. Miami,
   Sept. 11, 1994, 51 attempts.

30, Lynn Dickey, vs. Atlanta, Sept. 13, 1981, 44 attempts.
30, Don Majkowski, vs. Detroit, Nov. 20, 1988, 43 attempts.

Most Passes Attempted (career)
3,149, Bart Starr, 16 seasons.
2,831, Lynn Dickey, 9 seasons.
2,688, Brett Favre, 5 seasons.
1,854, Tobin Rote, 7 seasons.
1,607, Don Majkowski, 6 seasons.

Most Passes Attempted (season)
599, Don Majkowski, 1989.
582, Brett Favre, 1994.
570, Brett Favre, 1995.
543, Brett Favre, 1996.
522, Brett Favre, 1993.
492, Randy Wright, 1986.
484, Lynn Dickey, 1983.

Most Passes Attempted (game)
61, Brett Favre, vs. San Franciso, Oct. 14, 1997, completed 28.
59, Don Majkowski, at Detroit, Nov. 12, 1989, completed 34.
54, Brett Favre, at Chicago Bears, Dec. 5, 1993, completed 36.
54, Randy Wright, vs. San Francisco, Oct. 26, 1986, completed 30.
53, Don Majkowski, at Tampa Bay, Dec. 3, 1989, completed 25.
52, Randy Wright, at. Detroit, Dec. 4, 1988, completed 29.
51, Lynn Dickey, at Tampa Bay, Oct. 12, 1980, completed 35.
51, Randy Wright, at Tampa Bay, Oct. 2, 1988, completed 28.
51, Brett Favre, vs. Miami, Sept. 11, 1994, completed 31 & vs. St.
Louis Rams, Sept. 3, 1995, completed 29.

Fewest Passes Intercepted (season)
3, Bart Starr, 1966, 251 attempts.

Most Passes Intercepted (career)
151, Lynn Dickey, 9 seasons.
138, Bart Starr, 16 seasons.
119, Tobin Rote, 7 seasons.

90, Arnie Herber, 9 seasons.
77, Brett Favre, 5 seasons.
61, Babe Parilli, 4 seasons.

Most Passes Intercepted (season)
29, Lynn Dickey, 1983, 484 attempts.
25, Lynn Dickey, 1980, 478 attempts.
24, Tobin Rote, 1950, 224 attempts.
24, Brett Favre, 1993, 522 attempts.
23, Randy Wright, 1986, 492 attempts.
21, Irv Comp, 1944, 177 attempts.
21, Jack Jacobs, 1948, 184 attempts.
21, John Hadl, 1975, 353 attempts.

Most Passes Intercepted (game)
6, Tom O'Malley, vs. Detroit, Sept. 17, 1950, 15 attempts.

Most Consecutive Passes Thrown Without Interception
294, Bart Starr, 1964-65

Most Passes Attempted, Rookie (season)
224, Tobin Rote, 1950.
177, Babe Parilli, 1952.
163, Scott Hunter, 1971.
127, Don Majkowski, 1987.
106, Stan Heath, 1949.
105, David Whitehurst, 1977.

Most Passes Completed, Rookie (season)
83, Tobin Rote, 1950.
77, Babe Parilli, 1952.
75, Scott Hunter, 1971.
55, Don Majkowski, 1987.
50, David Whitehurst, 1977.

Yardage

Most Yards Gained on Passes (career)
23,718, Bart Starr, 16 seasons.
21,369, Lynn Dickey, 9 seasons.
18,724, Brett Favre, 5 seasons.
11,535, Tobin Rote, 7 seasons.
10,106, Don Majkowski, 6 seasons.

Most Yards Gained on Passes (season)
4,458, Lynn Dickey, 1983, 484 attempts.
4,413, Brett Favre, 1995, 570 attempts.
4,318, Don Majkowski, 1989, 599 attempts.
3,899, Brett Favre, 1996, 543 attempts.
3,882, Brett Favre, 1994, 582 attempts.
3,529, Lynn Dickey, 1980, 478 attempts.
3,303, Brett Favre, 1993, 522 attempts.
3,247, Randy Wright, 1986, 492 attempts.
3,227, Brett Favre, 1992, 471 attempts.
3,195, Lynn Dickey, 1984, 401 attempts.

Most Yards Gained on Passes (game)
418, Lynn Dickey, at Tampa Bay, Oct. 12, 1980, 35 completions.
410, Don Horn, vs. St. Louis Cardinals, Dec. 21, 1969, 22 completions.
402, Brett Favre, at Chicago Bears, Dec. 5, 1993, 36 completions.

Longest Completed Pass
99 yards, Brett Favre to Robert Brooks, at Chicago Bears, Sept. 11, 1995.
96 yards, Tobin Rote to Billy Grimes, vs. San Francisco, Dec. 10, 1950.
95 yards, Lynn Dickey to Steve Odom, at Minnesota, Oct. 2, 1977.
92 yards, Arnie Herber to Don Hutson, vs. Chicago Cardinals, Oct. 8, 1939.
91 yards, Bart Starr to Boyd Dowler, at Los Angeles Rams, Dec. 17, 1960.

Shortest Completed Pass
4 inches, Cecil Isbell to Don Hutson, vs. Cleveland Rams, Oct. 18, 1942

Most Yards Gained, Rookie (season)
1,416, Babe Parilli, 1952.
1,231, Tobin Rote, 1950.
1,210, Scott Hunter, 1971.
875, Don Majkowski, 1987.
662, Irv Comp, 1943.
656, Cecil Isbell, 1938.
634, David Whitehurst, 1977.

Most Games, 300 Yards Passing (career)
15, Lynn Dickey, 9 seasons.
14, Brett Favre, 5 seasons.
9, Don Majkowski, 6 seasons.
5, Bart Starr, 16 seasons.
2, Tobin Rote, 7 seasons.
2, Randy Wright, 5 seasons.

Most Games, 300 Yards Passing (season)
7, Brett Favre, 1995.
6, Don Majkowski, 1989.
5, Lynn Dickey, 1983.

Most Touchdown Passes (career)
152, Bart Starr, 16 seasons.
147, Brett Favre, 5 seasons.
133, Lynn Dickey, 9 seasons.
89, Tobin Rote, 7 seasons.
64, Arnie Herber, 12 seasons.
59, Cecil Isbell, 5 seasons.
56, Don Majkowski, 6 seasons.

Most Touchdown Passes (season)
39, Brett Favre, 1996.
38, Brett Favre, 1995.
33, Brett Favre, 1994.
32, Lynn Dickey, 1983.
27, Don Majkowski, 1989.
25, Lynn Dickey, 1984.

Most Touchdown Passes (game)
5, Cecil Isbell, vs. Chicago Cardinals, Nov. 1, 1942.
5, Don Horn, vs. St. Louis Cardinals, Dec. 21, 1969.
5, Lynn Dickey, at New Orleans Saints, Dec. 13, 1981.
5, Lynn Dickey, at Houston Oilers, Sept. 4, 1983.
5, Brett Favre, vs. Chicago Bears, Nov. 12, 1995.

Most Touchdown Passes, Rookie (season)
13, Babe Parilli, 1952
7, Cecil Isbell, 1938.
7 Irv Comp, 1943.
7, Tobin Rote, 1950.
7, Scott Hunter, 1971.

Most Consecutive Completions
18, Lynn Dickey, at Houston Oilers, Sept.4, 1983.
18, Don Majkowski, vs. New Orleans Saints, Sept. 17, 1989

PASS RECEIVING
Passes Caught

Most Passes Caught (career)
595, Sterling Sharpe, 7 seasons.
530, James Lofton, 9 seasons.
488, Don Hutson, 11 seasons.
448, Boyd Dowler, 11 seasons.
345, Max McGee, 12 seasons.

Most Passes Caught (season)
112, Sterling Sharpe, 1993, 16 games, 7.00 catches per game.
108, Sterling Sharpe, 1992, 16 games, 6.75 catches per game.
102, Robert Brooks, 1995, 16 games, 6.38 catches per game.
90, Sterling Sharpe, 1989, 16 games, 5.63 catches per game.
78, Edgar Bennett, 1994, 16 games, 4.88 catches per game.
74, Don Hutson, 1942, 11 games, 6.73 catches per game.
71, James Lofton, 1980, 16 games, 4.44 catches per game.
71, James Lofton, 1981, 16 games, 4.44 catches per game.

Most Passes Caught (game)
14, Don Hutson, at New York Giants, Nov. 22, 1942, 134 yards.
13, Don Hutson, vs. Cleveland Rams, Oct. 18, 1942, 209 yards.
12, Ken Payne, at Denver, Sept. 29, 1975, 167 yards.
12, Vince Workman, vs. Minnesota, Sept. 6, 1992, 50 yards.
11, Robert Brooks, vs. Pittsburgh, Dec. 24, 1994, 137 yards.
11, Don Beebe, vs. San Francisco, Oct. 14, 1996, 220 yards.
(Don Hutson, Bob Mann, Billy Howton, Eddie Lee Ivery, Gerry Ellis, James Lofton, and Sterling Sharpe have also caught 11 passes in a single game.)

Most Consecutive Games One or More Pass Receptions
103, Sterling Sharpe, from 10th game 1988 thru 16th game 1994.
60, Edgar Bennett, from 1st game 1993 thru 12th game 1996.
58, James Lofton.
50, Don Hutson.
50, Paul Coffman.

Pass Receiving Yardage
Most Yards Gained Catching Passes (career)
9,656, James Lofton, 9 seasons.
8,134, Sterling Sharpe, 7 seasons.
7,991, Don Hutson, 11 seasons.
6,918, Boyd Dowler, 11 seasons.
6,346, Max McGee, 12 seasons.
5,581, Billy Howton, 7 seasons.
5,422, Carroll Dale, 8 seasons.

Most Yards (season)
1,497, Robert Brooks, 1995.
1,461, Sterling Sharpe, 1992.
1,423, Sterling Sharpe, 1989.
1,361, James Lofton, 1984.
1,300, James Lofton, 1983.

Most Yards (game)
257, Bill Howton vs. Los Angeles Rams, Oct. 21, 1956, 7 receptions.

237, Don Hutson, at. Brooklyn, Nov. 21, 1943, 8 receptions.
220, Don Beebe, vs. San Francisco, Oct. 14, 1996, 11 receptions.
209, Don Hutson, vs. Cleveland Rams, Oct. 18, 1942, 13 receptions.
207, Don Hutson, vs. Chicago Cardinals, Nov. 1, 1942, 5 receptions & vs.
     Card-Pitt, Oct. 8, 1944, 11 receptions.
206, James Lofton, at Denver, Oct. 15, 1984, 11 receptions.
205, Carroll Dale, vs. Detroit, Sept. 29, 1968, 6 receptions.
200, Billy Howton, at Los Angeles, Dec.7, 1952, 6 receptions.

Most Passes Caught, Rookie (season)
55, Sterling Sharpe, 1988.
53, Billy Howton, 1952.
48, Gerry Ellis, 1980.
46, James Lofton, 1978.
39, Keith Woodside, 1988.

Most Yards Gained, Rookie (season)
1,231, Billy Howton, 1952.
818, James Lofton, 1978.
791, Sterling Sharpe, 1988.
614, Max McGee, 1954.
549, Boyd Dowler, 1959.

Touchdowns
Most Touchdown Passes Caught (career)
99, Don Hutson, 11, seasons.
65, Sterling Sharpe, 7 seasons.
50, Max McGee, 12, seasons.
49, James Lofton, 9 seasons.
43, Billy Howton, 7 seasons.

Most Touchdown Passes Caught (season)
18, Sterling Sharpe, 1994, 16 games.
17, Don Hutson, 1942, 11 games.
13, Billy Howton, 1952, 12 games.
13, Sterling Sharpe, 1992, 16 games.
13, Robert Brooks, 1995, 16 games.

Most Touchdown Passes Caught (game)
4, Don Hutson vs. Detroit Lions, Oct. 7, 1945
4, Sterling Sharpe, at Tampa Bay, Oct. 24, 1993 & at Dallas, Nov. 24, 1994.

Most Touchdown Passes Caught, Rookie (season)
13, Billy Howton, 1952.
9, Max McGee, 1954.
6, Don Hutson, 1935.
6, James Lofton, 1978.
5, Ray Pelfrey, 1951.
5, Carlton Elliott, 1951.

INTERCEPTIONS BY

Most Interceptions (career)
52, Bobby Dillon, 8 seasons.
48, Willie Wood, 12 seasons.
39, Her Adderly, 9 seasons.
33, Irv Comp, 7 seasons.
31, Mark Lee, 11 seasons.

Most Interceptions (season)
10, Irv Comp, 1943.
9, Bobby Dillon, 1953, 1955, 1957.
9, John Symank, 1957.
9, Willie Wood, 1962.
9, Willie Buchanan, 1978.
9, Tom Flynn, 1984.
9, Mark Lee, 1986.

Most Interceptions (game)
4, Bobby Dillon vs. Detroit Lions, Nov. 26, 1953.
4, Willie Buchanan vs. San Diego Chargers, Sept. 24, 1978.

Longest Interception Return
99 yards, Tim Lewis, vs. Los Angeles Rams, Nov. 18, 1984

94 yards, Rebel Steiner vs. Chicago Bears, Oct. 1, 1950.
91 yards, Hal Van Every, at Pittsburgh, Nov. 23, 1941.

Most Touchdowns (season)
3, Herb Adderly, 1965.

SCORING
Points
Most Points (career)
823, Don Hutson, 11 seasons.
820, Chris Jacke, 8 seasons.
760, Paul Hornung, 9 seasons.
546, Jim Taylor, 9 seasons.
521, Chester Marcol, 9 seasons.

Most Points (season)
176, Paul Hornung, 1960
146, Paul Hornung, 1961.
138, Don Hutson, 1942.
128, Chester Marcol, 1972.
128, Chris Jacke, 1993.

Most Points (game)
33, Paul Hornung, vs. Baltimore Colts, Oct. 8, 1961.
31, Don Hutson, vs. Detroit, Oct. 7, 1945.
30, Paul Hornung, at Baltimore Colts, Dec. 12, 1965.
28, Paul Hornung, vs. Minnesota, Sept. 16, 1993.

Most Points (one quarter)
29, Don Hutson vs. Detroit Lions, Oct. 7, 1945.

Most Points, No Touchdowns (season)
128, Chester Marcol, 1972.
128, Chris Jacke, 1993.
115, Jan Stenerud, 1983.
114, Chris Jacke, 1996.

Most Points, Rookie (season)
128, Chester Marcol, 1972
108, Chris Jacke, 1989.

Field Goals

Most Field Goals (career)
173, Chris Jacke, 8 seasons.
120, Chester Marcol, 9 seasons.
66, Paul Hornung, 9 seasons.
59, Jan Stenerud, 4 seasons.
53, Fred Cone, 7 seasons.
50, Al Del Greco, 4 seasons.

Most Field Goals (season)
33, Chester Marcol, 1972
31, Chris Jacke, 1993.
25, Chester Marcol, 1974.
23, Chris Jacke, 1990.
22, Jan Stenerud, 1981.
22, Chris Jacke, 1989 & 1992.
21, Chester Marcol, 1973.
21, Jan Stenerud, 1983.
21, Chris Jacke, 1996.

Most Field Goals (game)
5, Chris Jacke vs. Los Angeles Raiders, Nov. 11, 1990.

Longest Field Goal
54 yards, Chris Jacke, at Detroit, Jan. 2, 1994.
53 yards, Jan Stenerud, at Tampa Bay, Nov. 22, 1981.
53 yards, Chris Jacke, vs. Los Angeles Rams, Sept. 9, 1990; at New York Jets, Nov. 3, 1991; at Detroit, Nov. 1, 1992; vs. San Francisco, Oct. 14, 1996.

Most Field Goals Attempted (career)
224, Chris Jacke, 8 seasons.
195, Chester Marcol, 9 seasons.

128, Paul Hornung, 9 seasons.
98, Ted Fritsch, 9 seasons.
89, Fred Cone, 7 seasons.

Most Field Goals Attempted (season)
48, Chester Marcol, 1972
39, Chester Marcol, 1974.
38, Paul Hornung, 1964.
37, Chris Jacke, 1993.
35, Chester Marcol, 1973.

Most Field Goals, Rookie (season)
33, Chester Marcol, 1972.
22, Chris Jacke, 1989.
11, Joe Danelo, 1975.

Most Consecutive Games Scoring Field Goals
12, Jan Stenerud, 1980-81.
12, Chris Jacke, 1991-92.
10, Fed Cone, 1955.
10, Chris Jacke, 1989-90 & 1993.

Most Consecutive Field Goals
17, Chris Jacke, 1993.
15, Chris Jacke, 1989-90.
11, Jan Stenerud, 1981.
10, Max Zendejas, 1987.

Points After Touchdown
Most PATs Attempted (career)
306, Chris Jacke, 8 seasons.
214, Fred Cone, 7 seasons.
194, Paul Hornung, 9 seasons.
184, Don Hutson, 11 seasons.
164, Chester Marcol, 9 seasons.

Most PATs Attempted (season)
53, Chris Jacke, 1996.
52, Jan Stenerud, 1983.
46, Jerry Kramer, 1963.
43, Paul Hornung, 1964.
43, Don Chandler, 1966.
43, Chris Jacke, 1994 & 1995.
42, Chris Jacke, 1989.

Most PATs (career)
301, Chris Jacke, 8 seasons.
200, Fred Cone, 7 seasons.
190, Paul Hornung, 9 seasons.
172, Don Hutson, 11 seasons.
155, Chester Marcol, 9 seasons.

Most PATs (season)
52, Jan Stenerud, 1983, 52 attempts.
51, Chris Jacke, 1996, 53 attempts.
43, Jerry Kramer, 1963, 46 attempts.
43, Chris Jacke, 1995, 43 attempts.
42, Chris Jacke, 1989, 42 attempts.

Most PATs (game)
8, Don Chandler vs. Atlanta, Oct. 23, 1966.
7, Don Hutson, vs. Detroit, Oct. 7, 1945.
7, Paul Hornung, at Cleveland, Oct. 15, 1961 & vs. Chicago, Sept. 30, 1962.
7, Jerry Kramer, at Philadelphia, Nov. 11, 1962.
7, Don Chandler, vs. Cleveland, Nov. 12, 1967.
7, Jan Stenerud, vs. Tampa Bay, Oct. 2, 1983.

Most Consecutive PATs
134, Chris Jacke, 1990-94
99, Paul Hornung, 1960-62, 1964.
74, Al Del Greco, 1985-87.
67, Jan Stenerud, 1982-83.
62, Don Hutson, 1942-44.

PACKERS
VS.
NFL OPPONENTS

Some compilers of Packer records against other teams in the NFL have made mistakes and/or have taken liberties with history. The Packer media guide once contained such errors, but they have corrected them over the past few years. Not so the media guides of some other NFL teams that I've had the opportunity to examine in recent years. The worst example I've seen so far is the 1996 guide of the St. Louis Rams.

Some current franchises have played in a myriad of cities and had several nicknames, such as the Indianapolis Colts who have been the Baltimore Colts, Dallas Texans, and New York Yanks. However, the Baltimore Colts of 1950 was not the same franchise. That franchise came from the All-America Conference when the two leagues merged in 1950. After one year, Baltimore lost its franchise completely, and its players were dispersed to the remaining 12 teams, including the

New York Yanks who were actually a combination of the former New York Bulldogs of the NFL and the Boston Yanks of the AAC.

Adding to the confusion is the circumstance surrounding the Philadelphia Eagles, Chicago Cardinals, and Pittsburgh Steelers during World War II. Because of a lack of playing talent, the Eagles and Steelers merged for 1943 as the Phil-Pitt Steagles and the Cardinals and the Steelers merged for 1944 and were known simply as Card-Pitt.

Technically speaking, the Chicago Staleys and Decatur Staleys were not the Chicago Bears. The Staley franchise was surrendered to the league at the January, 1922 winter meeting, and George Halas and his partners were granted a new franchise known as the Chicago Bears the next day. Of course, the same technicality applies to the Packers because the Clairs surrendered their franchise to the NFL at the same meeting and Curly Lambeau wasn't granted a new one until that summer.

Considering all that history, I found it easier to compile the Packers' record against all of their NFL opponents by city and nickname instead of by franchise only. Of course, the exceptions are the Baltimore Colts, Boston Braves/Redskins, and Brooklyn Dodgers/Tigers. The Colts were actually two different teams and franchises in history, while the Dodgers and Braves merely changed their nicknames.

To make matters worse for modern historians and compilers, the Cleveland Browns no longer exist, their owner, Art "I can't make an honest buck by Lake Erie" Modell, having shifted his franchise to Baltimore and giving the team a new nickname, the Ravens. Also, the Houston Oilers are soon to move to Tennessee, and their city name as well as nickname are still in doubt. The Seattle Seahawks want to move to Los Angeles, which is currently without a team. What will they become if they should move? And what will the next Los Angeles team be called?

Then there's Al Davis who plays musical cities. He takes his franchise wherever he pleases, whenever it pleases him. First Oakland, then LA, now Oakland again. He'd probably move his team to Yuba City, Arizona, if the Navajo Nation would build him a stadium with enough luxury boxes in it. Rumor has it that his business card reads:

> *Have NFL Franchise, Will Travel.*
> *Call Al Davis*
> ~~*Oakland*~~
> ~~*Los Angeles*~~
> *Oakland*

What's a modern historian to do? Just go with the flow and keep racking up those cities and nicknames.

Thank God and Gerald Clifford that the Packers are still right where they belong, and thank the fans that they still have the nickname of Packers instead of the Blues like Curly Lambeau wanted back in 1922 when he was awarded a franchise for Green Bay. Clifford was the attorney who set up the non-profit corporation that operates the Packers, and he's the one who stuck in the clause that the franchise couldn't be sold or moved without the approval of the stockholders. And when Lambeau began calling his team the Blues in 1922, the fans ignored him and kept calling them the Packers. Good for them and now us.

REGULAR SEASON OPPONENTS	W	L	T
Arizona Cardinals	0	0	0
Atlanta Falcons	10	9	0
Baltimore Colts (first)	0	1	0
Baltimore Colts (second)	17	16	1
Baltimore Ravens	0	0	0
Boston Braves/Redskins	4	1	1
Boston Yanks	3	0	0
Brooklyn Dodgers/Tigers	10	0	0
Buffalo Bills	1	5	0
Card-Pitt	2	0	0
Carolina Panthers	0	0	0
Chicago Bears	65	80	6
Chicago Cardinals	31	19	3
Chicago Staleys	0	1	0
Cincinnati Bengals	4	4	0
Cincinnati Reds	1	0	0
Cleveland Browns	8	6	0
Cleveland Bulldogs	1	0	0
Cleveland Indians	1	0	0
Cleveland Rams	12	3	1
Columbus Panhandles	1	0	0
Dallas Cowboys	8	9	0
Dallas Texans	2	0	0
Dayton Triangles	5	0	0
Denver Broncos	3	4	1
Detroit Lions	65	56	6
Detroit Panthers	2	0	0
Duluth Eskimos	1	0	1
Duluth Kellys	2	1	0
Evansville Crimson Giants	1	0	0
Frankford Yellow Jackets	5	4	1
Hammond Pros	3	0	0
Houston Oilers	3	3	0
Indianapolis Colts	1	2	0
Jacksonville Jaguars	1	0	0

Kansas City Blues	2	0	0
Kansas City Chiefs	1	5	1
Los Angeles Raiders	2	2	0
Los Angeles Rams	25	39	1
Louisville Colonels	1	0	0
Miami Dolphins	0	8	0
Milwaukee Badgers	9	0	1
Minneapolis Marines	4	0	0
Minneapolis Red Jackets	4	0	0
Minnesota Vikings	34	36	1
New England Patriots	2	3	0
New Orleans Saints	13	4	0
New York Bulldogs	1	0	0
New York Giants	22	20	2
New York Jets	2	5	0
New York Yankees	1	0	1
New York Yanks	1	3	0
Oakland Raiders	0	3	0
Philadelphia Eagles	20	8	0
Phil-Pitt Steagles	1	0	0
Phoenix Cardinals	2	0	0
Pittsburgh Pirates/Steelers	18	11	0
Portsmouth Spartans	3	2	1
Pottsville Maroons	1	2	0
Providence Steam Roller	4	0	1
Racine Legion	3	3	1
Racine Tornadoes	1	0	0
Rochester Jeffersons	1	0	0
Rock Island Independents	1	3	1
St. Louis All-Stars	1	0	0
St. Louis Cardinals	6	2	1
St. Louis Gunners	2	0	0
St. Louis Rams	1	1	0
San Diego Chargers	5	1	0
San Francisco 49ers	22	25	1
Seattle Seahawks	4	3	0

Staten Island Stapletons	5	0	0
Tampa Bay Buccaneers	22	13	1
Tennessee Oilers	0	0	0
Washington Redskins	9	11	0

POST-SEASON OPPONENTS

	W	L
Atlanta Falcons	1	0
Baltimore Colts (second)	1	0
Boston Redskins	1	0
Carolina Panthers	1	0
Chicago Bears	0	1
Cleveland Browns	2	0
Dallas Cowboys	2	4
Detroit Lions	2	0
Kansas City Chiefs	1	0
Los Angeles Rams	1	0
New England Patriots	1	0
New York Giants	4	1
Oakland Raiders	1	0
Philadelphia Eagles	0	1
St. Louis Cardinals	1	1
San Francisco 49ers	2	0
Washington Redskins	0	1

PACKER TRIVIA

CRAIG NEWSOME

THE LAMBEAU YEARS QUIZ

REGGIE WHITE

1
BEFORE THEY WERE PACKERS

The Earliest Green Bay Team.
Professional football in the city of Green Bay began long before the founding of the National Football League. The first city team in Green Bay began play before Curly Lambeau was even born, and the roster was made up of local players and a manager who passed a hat through the crowd to collect donations for the team.

1. What year did this historic town eleven first take the field?

2. Who was their first opponent?

3. What was the outcome?

4. Where was did the Green Bay town team play home games in those earliest years?

5. Name three Wisconsin cities that Green Bay played in 1896.

6. What was the team's won-lost record in 1896?

7. How many points did the Green Bay squad score in 1896?

8. Who were the players for this first team? Last names are all that is necessary because the newspapers of the day seldom printed first names.

Later Green Bay City Teams.
Green Bay has always been a proud city with a history reaching back to the 17th Century when the first French explorers visited the area. Vince Lombardi's immortal words, "Winning isn't everything; it's the only thing!" aptly described the attitude of the city's earliest settlers, and this credo was carried onto the athletic field. To give his town the best team possible, the organizer of the second city team

hired Green Bay's first professional football player.

Winning football teams became another source of pride for Green Bay in succeeding years. Town teams took on all comers, and they gave no quarter, expecting none in return. Even the city league, which produced the players for the town team, was highly competitive.

9. Who organized the third pro team in Green Bay?

10. What year did this team play in Green Bay?

11. Who was the first professional player for Green Bay?

12. What was the won-lost record of the third team?

13. Where did the third team play its games?

14. Who sponsored the 1915 city team?

15. What was the last year that Green Bay did *not* have a city team between the year of the first team and the formation of the Packers?

16. Name some of the teams in the city league.

A Prominent Early Football Family.

Green Bay has always been an ethnic melting pot. People from dozens of countries around the world have settled there over the years, from the French to the latest arrivals from the Orient, the Hmong. Three Jewish brothers from Russia came in the 19th Century, and four members of that family's second generation became very prominent in the early days of Green Bay football history. They were two sets of brothers and cousins.

17. What was the original spelling of this Jewish family's last name?

18. Which cousin held the post of business manager for the 1905 city team?

19. Which three cousins played on some of the city teams?

20. Which cousin sponsored his own team in the city league?

21. Which cousin played for the Packers in the NFL?

22. Which cousin organized and backed the 1918 town team?

23. What were the nicknames of the 1918 team?

24. Who was the business manager of the 1918 team?

Bonus Questions

25. Who is given credit for bringing professional football to Green Bay in 1895?

26. Who captained the second pro team in Green Bay in 1896?

2
THE PACKERS BEFORE THE NFL

Organizing the Packers.

Professional football had been proliferating all over the country before World War I as every town that could put 11 men on the field came up with a team. After the war, the game moved from being a club sport to more serious competition between larger towns hiring the best players to the first organized league, the American Professional Football Association.

In Wisconsin, a mythical state championship became the prize for the pro teams. Not all teams competed for the title, but Green Bay did. To that end, the best team possible was brought together thanks to the efforts of a single newspaper reporter.

1. What is the exact date of the first organizational meeting of the city team that came to be known as the Green Bay Packers?

2. Where was this meeting held?

3. What is the exact date of the second organizational meeting of the city team that came to be known as the Green Bay Packers?

4. What was the most significant decision made at the second meeting?

5. What was the other important decision made at the second meeting?

6. What company agreed to sponsor the city team for that year?

7. What was the name of the executive who agreed to sponsor the city team?

8. What was the first nickname given to the city team after the second organizational meeting?

9. Who dubbed the city team the Packers?

The First City Team Known as the Packers.
    The Green Bay city teams had been playing squads from all over northeastern Wisconsin and the Upper Peninsula of Michigan for more than two decades before they got a corporate sponsor and became the Packers. This changed drastically this first season that the team was known as the Packers. Their captain arranged several games with the best aggregations from outside the area just to prove that his team was the best in the state. This was the beginning of the Packer legend.

10. What was the won-lost record of this first Packer team?

11. Which three teams from the Upper Peninsula did the Packers play that first season?

12. What four city teams from Wisconsin did the Packers play that first season?

13. What two club teams did the Packers play that first season?

14. Which Packer opponent was sponsored by the local American Legion post?

15. Which team did the Packers play for the mythical Wisconsin state championship after the conclusion of their "regular season" schedule?

16. What business sponsored this championship opponent?

17. What was the outcome of this so-called title game?

18. What was the price of ticket to Packer games that year?

The Second City Team Known as the Packers.

A professional football association was formed in another state during the late summer of following year, but none of the pro teams in Wisconsin was informed of the meeting and asked to join the organization. By the time word of the new group spread to Green Bay, the opportunity for Lambeau and Calhoun to get the Packers had passed; therefore, Lambeau determined to prepare his squad for the next year by crushing as many opponents as possible that year and thus enhance Green Bay's reputation as the best eleven in Wisconsin.

On the home front, the Green Bay city team was forced to find a new sponsor when their previous benefactor sold out to another company. As it turned out, this was a blessing in disguise.

19. What was the name of the team's new sponsor?

20. Who was the executive who put his company's money behind the city team?

21. Which two teams did the Packers play twice in their second season?

22. Which two traditional opponents did the Packers play that year?

23. Which two "big city" athletic clubs did the Packers play that year?

24. Who were the Milwaukee "All-Stars"?

25. Which three opponents managed to score on the Packers that year?

3
THE PACKERS JOIN THE NFL

Before the National Football League.
For several decades, George Halas was considered to be "the" authority on the earliest years of the National Football League. True historians of the game have proven Halas had one of those convenient, self-serving memories; convenient in that none of those tales of yore related any of his less reputable business dealings and self-serving in that he recalled only events that made him look good. Of course, Halas wasn't alone; most of his contemporaries, including and especially Curly Lambeau, stood side-by-side on the same self-aggrandizing pedestal.

1. What was the name of the first professional football organization?

2. When was this organization founded?

3. Where was this organization founded?

4. Name the 11 cities that were represented at the organizational meeting.

5. Who was the first president of the organization?

The Packers Join the Big Boys.
Although he missed getting the Packers into the original organization in its first year, Curly Lambeau was determined to get Green Bay into the circuit the next year. Much to his chagrin, the loop folded short-ly after its inaugural season. When its leaders met the following spring, to reorganize, Lambeau was again unaware of their gathering, and he missed another chance to join the real pros.

A third opportunity arose later that summer when Calhoun heard in advance about another meeting of the National Football League organizers. He told Lambeau about it, and the man who put the Packers on the map of professional football took the next step. He told his boss about the pro circuit and how good it would be for Green Bay to join it. The boss agreed, and he sent his brother to the next meeting of the NFL to request a franchise for Green Bay.

6. What was the name of the company that sponsored the Green Bay team in its first year in the NFL?

7. Who was granted a franchise to field a team in the city of Green Bay, Wisconsin, for the second season of the NFL?

8. When was this franchise granted?

9. Who were the four "non-conference" opponents to face the Packers before Green Bay began playing the real pros?

10. Who was the very first opponent for the Packers in their initial season in the pro league?

11. Which three teams did the Packers defeat consecutively at home?

12. Who did the Packers play their first road contest against in the professional league?

13. Who was the final professional opponent for the Packers that first year in the NFL?

14. Who was Green Bay's opponent in challenge match for the mythical state championship?

The Packers Get the Boot.
One of the first rules of the APFA when it was formed was "hands off college players." In other words, no team could sign a college player until his college days had expired. The reason for this rule was born out of a desire to get along with the sportswriters of the time because the fledgling league needed their support to draw fans to

games. Since most of the scribes favored the college game over the professional version, this was a difficult task at best.

To show the newspapermen that they meant business with the rule, the pro magnates never hesitated to blow the whistle on any small town team that used college players. A game between two town teams in Illinois really raised hell for the pros when it was discovered that one team employed a bunch of players from the University of Illinois and the other used a group from Notre Dame. Arch Ward of the Chicago *Tribune* led the chorus in berating the pros for tainting these fine young men with money, but he wasn't satisfied because there was little to nothing that anybody could do to the local yokels down state.

The same wasn't true when Curly Lambeau employed three college boys to play for the Packers.

15. Against which team did Lambeau use college players?

16. Which college were these players attending at the time?

17. Which of the three players had played out his college football eligibility but still had plans to play hockey in school?

18. Who blew the whistle on Lambeau for using college players?

19. What was the result of Lambeau being caught using college players?

20. What did Lambeau do at the league meeting that dealt with his use of college players?

21. What persistent action did Lambeau take that next summer?

22. What was Lambeau's reward for his persistence?

Lambeau's Corporation.

A lot of fanciful tales about Curly Lambeau came out of the college player episode. One of them had his good friend Neil Murphy selling his car to help Lambeau get the franchise for Green Bay. It's a pretty good yarn, but the real truth tells more about Lambeau and the people of Green Bay.

23. What was the name of Lambeau's corporation?

24. Who were the other incorporators of this business?

25. What tough decision did the incorporators have to make on Thanksgiving Day that season?

26. Who advised them on what to do that day?

27. What did incorporators do?

28. What promise was made to the incorporators?

The First Non-Profit Corporation.
   The businesspeople of Green Bay rescued professional football for the people of northeast Wisconsin when they formed a new corporation that took over operation of the Packers the next season. They bought stock in this company knowing fully that they would never get their money back, that they would never realize a profit from the venture. They didn't care about the money; they cared about their town and its football team.

29. Who was the lawyer who set up this non-profit corporation?

30. What was the name of this new corporation?

31. Who were the community leaders behind this organization?

32. What the price of a share of stock in this corporation?

33. How many stockholders would comprise the board of directors for the new corporation?

34. Who was elected as the first president of this corporation?

35. Who were the members of the first executive committee of the

corporation?

36. What part did the owners of the former corporation that operated Lambeau's franchise have in the new organization?

4
A FEW GOOD MEN

Earl Louis Lambeau.

One of the most enigmatic men in the history of the National Football League. That best describes Earl Louis Lambeau, better known as Curly because of his naturally curly black hair. He was man and myth, fact and legend. A great athlete in high school, good enough to play first string fullback as college freshman, the leader of his home-town team against other town teams, a fair player as a pro, a coach whose best ability lie in recognizing talent in players and convincing them to play in tiny Green Bay, Wisconsin. As a man, he was what Texans and Oklahomans call "a good ol' boy"—a likeable guy with the morals of an alley cat and the scruples of a Ferengi businessman. He made history, and what history he didn't make, he made up.

1. When was he born?

2. What was his father's first name?

3. What business was his father in?

4. What nationality were the Lambeaus?

5. Which Green Bay high school did Curly attend?

6. What was the first college that he attended?

7. What was the second college that he attended?

8. Who was the famous halfback that played alongside Lambeau in college?

9. Who was his college football coach?

10. Why did he leave college?

11. Who did he marry?

12. What was Curly's job at the packing plant?

13. When was he inducted into the Pro Football Hall of Fame?

14. When was he inducted into the Packer Hall of Fame?

George Whitney Calhoun.

John Torinus, Sr., probably knew Calhoun better than anybody. In his work on the Packers, *The Packer Legend: An Inside Look* (Laranmark Press, 1982), he wrote about the man who took young Torinus under his wing and made him into one of the more notable journalists in the history of Wisconsin. Just as importantly, Calhoun took the Packers under his wing and made them into a legend.

15. When was Cal born?

16. Who was Cal's famous Green Bay ancestor?

17. Where did Cal attend college?

18. What sports did Cal play in college?

19. What changed Cal's life from a career in sports to a career in journalism?

20. What was the name of the newspaper where Cal worked?

21. What was Cal's connection to the town team and later the Packers?

22. When was Cal inducted into the Packer Hall of Fame?

Andrew B. Turnbull.

   Men of foresight are rare. Men of foresight and action are even harder to find. Men of foresight, action, and determination come along only once in a great while. If not for Turnbull, the Packers would be a mere footnote in the football encyclopedias.

23. Where was he born?

24. When did he come to Green Bay?

25. Where did he work in Green Bay?

26. What position did he hold with his employer?

27. What position did he hold with the Packers?

28. When was he inducted into the Packer Hall of Fame?

Leland Joannes, Gerald Clifford, W. Weber Kelly.

   Milwaukee *Journal* sportswriter Ollie Kuechle dubbed Lambeau, Turnbull, Joannes, Clifford, and Kelly "the Hungry Five" because they seemed to be asking for money for the Packers all the time. Most visible among them was Lambeau, and close behind the man on the field was the top man in the office, Turnbull. Although they remained out of the spotlight, no one who knows the Packer story can deny the major contributions that this trio made to the preservation of the Packers in the NFL.

29. Where was Clifford born?

30. Where was Kelly born?

31. What business was Joannes in?

32. What post did Clifford hold in the corporation?

33. Why did Kelly resign from the executive committee?

34. How long was Joannes president of the corporation?

35. When was Joannes inducted into the Packer Hall of Fame?

36. How long did Kelly serve as president of the corporation?

37. When was Clifford inducted into the Packer Hall of Fame?

38. What monumental contribution to the Packers did Clifford make?

5
THE FIRST TRIPLE CHAMPS

Getting There, Part 1.

Curly Lambeau realized right from the start that winning mythical state championships could be done with local talent, but to be a winner in a professional league that consisted of hired teams from all over the Midwest, he had to find talent outside the Green Bay area. His 1921 squad had only a few men who had played on big-time college programs. He brought in more outside talent for the '22 team, and the '23 roster could compete with any in the league. As the rest of the league progressed, Lambeau kept one step ahead of the competition.

1. Who was the first star player from outside the Green Bay area to sign with the Packers?

2. Who was the first integral part of the "First Triple Champs" to join the Packers?

3. Who was the center that Lambeau signed to play for the Packers in the middle of the '22 season and who stayed with Green Bay into the championship years?

4. Who was the last player from the 1919 team, besides Lambeau, to play

for the Packers after Green Bay joined the NFL?

5. Who was the home-grown back who played his college ball at Indiana and signed with the Packers in 1922?

6. What were the won-lost-tied records of Lambeau's first three NFL teams? (League record only.)

Getting There, Part 2.

With each passing season, the professional game became more acceptable to the sporting public. Attendance increased, and so did the size of rosters and salaries.

Lambeau had the beginnings of a championship team, but the nucleus was still incomplete. He needed more star players. He added two in 1924 and one each in 1925 and 1926 to bring the Packers closer to their first title.

7. Who was the triple-threat back that Lambeau signed in 1924 and stayed with the Packers through the championship years?

8. Who was the guard that joined the Packers in 1924 and played on the first two championship teams?

9. Who was the back that signed with the Packers in 1925 and played on the first championship team?

10. Who was the fullback that Lambeau added to his title recipe in 1926?

11. What were the won-lost-tied records and finishes for Lambeau's next three NFL teams?

Getting There, Part 3.

Now that he had the core Lambeau needed some meat for his football apple. He picked up most of it for the '27 and '28 seasons by signing seven players who played important roles on the '29 champions. The most vital position he filled at this time was field general when he found the quarterback who made the Packers into real winners.

12. Who were the three college interior linemen that Lambeau signed in 1927, two of whom played on all three title teams while the third played only on the '29 squad?

13. Who was the Packer Hall of Fame end that Lambeau acquired in 1927 after his former pro team folded?

14. What two NFL teams had Red Dunn played for before signing with the Packers in 1927?

15. Who were the two professional linemen that Lambeau signed in 1927, both of whom played only on the '29 champs?

16. Who was the end from Georgia to sign with the Packers in 1928?

17. What were the won-lost-tied records and finishes for the Packers in 1927 and 1928?

The First of Three Champions.

Just about everybody who knows anything about the Packers first triple champs can rattle off the names of Cal Hubbard, Mike Michalske, and the unforgettable Johnny Bloody. But they weren't the only prime football beef to join the Packers in 1929 and make little Green Bay, Wisconsin, the capital of the pro football world. Many historians have overlooked the contributions of Hurdis McCrary and Bo Molenda to those title teams.

18. Where had Hubbard played pro football before joining the Packers in 1929?

19. Where did Hubbard go to college?

20. What other sports profession did Hubbard enter after his football playing days were over?

21. What honors have been bestowed on Hubbard that no other sports figure is ever likely to achieve?

22. Where did Michalske go to college?

23. Where did Michalske play pro football before joining the Packers in 1929?

24. What is Michalske's real first name?

25. What is Johnny Blood's real name?

26. How did Johnny Blood get his nickname?

27. Where did Blood attend college?

28. Where did Blood play pro football before signing with the Packers in 1929?

29. What other pro team did Blood play for after the Packers?

30. Where did Hurdis McCrary go to college?

31. Where did Bo Molenda play pro football before joining the Packers in 1929?

32. Where did Molenda play college football?

33. Where did Molenda play after leaving the Packers?

34. What was the Packers' record in 1929?

The Second Champions.
    Elmer Sleight, Wuert Englemann, and a native son joined the Pack in 1930. Sleight and Englemann made major contributions to the team in the years they were with the Packers, but the native son made an impact on professional football.

35. Who was this native son who joined the Packers in 1930?

36. Where did this native son play some college football before dropping out to join the Packers?

37. What year was this native son inducted into the Pro Football Hall of Fame?

38. Where did Sleight go to college?

39. Where did Englemann go to college?

40. What was the Packers' record for 1930?

The First Triple Champions in NFL History.

When the Packers won their third straight NFL crown in 1931, they established a new standard for excellence in professional football. Their record over the four seasons of 1929-32 was a combined 44-8-3 for a percentage of .846 not counting the ties and .827 counting the ties. Few teams have ever come close to that kind of consistent winning.

Lambeau signed several new players to the roster for 1931, and four of them played prominent roles in the Packers' success. Two were backs, two were linemen, and two were from the Big Ten. These four major contributors to Green Bay's '31 title were Milt Gantenbein, Hank Bruder, Rudy Comstock, and Roger Grove.

41. Which two '31 signees were voted into the Packer Hall of Fame in 1972?

42. Which two '31 signees attended Big Ten colleges?

43. Which two '31 signees played on the line?

44. What college did Comstock attend?

45. What was the Packers' record for 1931?

The Year That Should Have Been.

If ties had counted in the 1930s, Green Bay would have won the NFL crown for the fourth year in a row. Ties didn't count; the Packers finished third in 1932 behind the Bears and Portsmouth who tied for first with 7-1-6 and 7-1-4 records respectively. The Packers lost their last two games of the year; to the Spartans in Portsmouth and to the Bears in Chicago. Had they won those— Aw, never mind. Talking about it won't change what's already water over the dam. Or is that under the bridge?

46. What was the Packers' record for 1932?

47. What was the Packers' consolation prize for another successful season?

48. What part did Johnny Blood play in the answer to the previous question?

49. What was Blood's other duty besides player in answer to question 47?

50. What famous Bear and former Illinois player joined the Packers for the second half of the answer to question 47?

6
THE HUTSON ERA

Rebuilding the Champs.
After a dozen seasons of winning football in the NFL, Green Bay fell short of the mark for the very first time in 1933. Why? Red Dunn and Vern Lewellen. Both had retired; Dunn after the '31 season and Lewellen after '32. They were sorely missed; not only for their football talents, but also for their leadership. These two men weren't simply superb players; they were also great people, outstanding individuals who would and did know success off the gridiron as well as on it. When they retired, the Packer house felt an emptiness it wouldn't feel again until 1946.

The '33 season was also the beginning of a new era for the NFL. The Bears and Portsmouth Spartans played the first championship game in the league's history at the end of the '32 season, and the interest this generated led to the first of many major changes in the NFL. The greatest of which was the alignment of the teams into two divisions. The others were changes in the rules that made the pro game distinctive from that of the colleges.

1. What was the result of the playoff game between the Bears and the Spartans?

2. Where was the game played?

3. What changes in the rules for the pros came about as a result of the Bears-Spartans playoff game?

4. What was the Packers' record for 1933?

5. What major catastrophe befell the corporation in 1933?

6. How did the corporation escape total destruction by this catastrophe?

7. What was the final result of this catastrophe?

The New Packers.
   Lambeau added several new faces to the Packers in 1933. Among them were Ben Smith, Joe Kurth, Jess Quatse, Norm Greeney, Lon Evans, Al Sarafiny, Paul Young, Bob Monnett, Buckets Goldenberg, and Buster Mott. He followed this by signing Joe Laws, Adolph "Tar" Schwammel, Bob Jones, Champ Seibold, Chester "Swede" Johnston, Carl Jorgensen, Frank Butler, Charley Casper, Al Norgard, Paul "Tiny" Engebretsen, and Harry Wunsch in 1934; George Maddox, Ernie Smith, George Sauer, Herm Schneidman, Bob Tenner, Dominic Vairo, Bob O'Connor, George Svendsen, and—oh, yes—Don Hutson in 1935; and Russ Letlow, Wayland Becker, Tony Paulekas, Bernie Scherer, Paul Miller, Cal Clemens, Harry Mattos, and Lou Gordon in 1936.
   Some of these men would only be around for a year. Some would be voted into the Packer Hall of Fame. All of them contributed to the rebuilding of the championship team from Green Bay in one way or

another.

8. Which of the new Packers of 1933 would one day be inducted into the Packer Hall of Fame?

9. Which of the '33 class of Packers were linemen?

10. Which of the '33 signees would play on the '36 championship team?

11. Which of the new Packers of 1934 would one day be inducted into the Packer Hall of Fame?

12. Which of the '34 class of Packers were backs?

13. Which of the '34 signees would play on the '36 championship team?

14. Which of the new Packers of 1935 would one day be inducted into the Packer Hall of Fame?

15. Which of the '35 class of Packers were linemen?

16. Which of the '35 signees would play on the '36 championship team?

17. Which of the new Packers of 1936 would one day be inducted into the Packer Hall of Fame?

18. Which of the '36 class of Packers were backs?

19. In their methodical climb back to the top, where did the Packers finish in the division standings in 1934 and 1935?

20. What were the Packers records for 1934, 1935, and 1936?

The Pack Was Back.

    Curly Lambeau had built the greatest football machine in the NFL's short history thru 1932, then saw it fall apart from age and injury in 1933. But within three years, he reconstructed the Packers and put Green Bay back on top of the pro football world. Over the 10-

year span of 1935 thru 1944, the Packers finished in first or second place in the Western Division, winning the division outright four times, tying for first once, and winning three NFL titles. Their total regular season record was 81-25-4 for a winning percentage of .755 (including ties as half a win and half a loss).

Over this same time period, the Bears finished first in the West five times, second, three times, and third twice. Not as good as the Packers. Chicago's record was 81-24-5 for a winning percentage of .757. The Redskins' record was 68-35-6, and the Giants' record was 70-31-9. Either the Giants or the Redskins won the Eastern Division every one of those years.

Although the Bears record was better and the Redskins and the Giants won more division titles than the Packers, Lambeau's teams were the most consistent in never finishing any lower than second place in that 10-year span. How many modern teams can say that? Very few, but not one of those teams played in the same division with another powerhouse team like the Bears of the same era.

With the retirements of several great Packers, Lambeau found some solid replacements through the college draft and through trades and free agency. In 1937, Eddie Jankowski, Averell Daniell, Earl Svendsen, Ray Peterson, Lyle Sturgeon, Darrell Lester, Herb Banet, and Francis "Zud" Schwammel joined the Packers. In 1938, Cecil Isbell, Andy Uram, Pete Tinsley, Buford "Baby" Ray, and Carl Mulleneaux put on the Packer colors. In 1939, all-time Packer greats Charley Brock and Larry Craig signed contracts with the Packers, as did Larry Buhler, Frank Steen, Frank Balazs, Tom Greenfield, John Biolo, Dick Zoll, and Harry Jacunski.

The Packers finished second in '37, won the Western Division in '38 and '39, and captured the NFL title in '39. Green Bay was the best team in the NFL over the four-year stretch of 1936 thru 1939.

21. Which of the new Packers of 1937 would one day be inducted into the Packer Hall of Fame?

22. Which of the '37 class of Packers were backs?

23. Which of the '37 signees would play on the '39 championship team?

24. Which of the new Packers of 1938 would one day be inducted into the Packer Hall of Fame?

25. Which of the '38 class of Packers were linemen?

26. Which of the '38 signees would play on the '39 championship team?

27. Which of the new Packers of 1939 would one day be inducted into the Packer Hall of Fame?

28. Which of the '39 class of Packers were backs?

29. What were the Packers records for 1937, 1938, and 1939?

Lambeau's Last Hurrah.
     The Packers slipped in a big way in 1940, but they did finish second. Two tough losses and a tie in the second half of the season cost them another division crown. This was the year the Bears annihilated the Redskins in the league title game by the most lopsided score in NFL history, regular season or playoffs, 73-0.
     Lambeau's crew had their third best ever regular season record in 1941, topped only by the '29 finish and the '62 mark. Even so, they wound up a bridesmaid. The same thing happened again in '42 and '43 as World War II depleted the ranks of the pro teams.
     With a nucleus that had been in Green Bay since before the war, Lambeau directed the Packers to their last championship under his tutelage in 1944. Green Bay did add a few new faces during this time. Lou Brock was drafted out of Purdue in 1940. Ed Frutig and Tony Canedeo emerged to prominence with the Packers from the '41 draft. Bill Kuusisto and Alex Urban were free agents out of college that made the '41 squad. Lambeau picked up Mike Bucchianeri from the Eagles in a trade before the season. Ted Fritsch signed as a free agent in '42, as did Ben Starrett, Joel Mason, Bob Kahler, Paul Berezney, Milburn Croft, and Bob Flowers. Irv Comp and Roy McKay came out of the '43 draft, and Forest McPherson, Glen Sorenson, and Don

Perkins signed as free agents. Lambeau signed free agents Paul Duhart, Ray Wehba, Bob Kercher, Dick Bilda, and Charley Tollefson for the '44 campaign.

30. Of this group of players who signed with the Packers in the years of 1940-44, which ones were inducted into the Packer Hall of Fame?

31. Where did Ted Fritsch go to college?

32. Where did Irv Comp go to college?

33. Which of the class of '42 Packers were linemen?

34. Which of the class of '43 Packers were backs?

35. Which of the class of '44 Packers were linemen?

36. What were the records of Green Bay's teams from 1940 thru 1944?

Clarke Hinkle.

During the '20s, the Packers had several great backs who played for them. Verne Lewellen, Charley Mathys, Eddie Kotal, Myrt Basing, and Curly Lambeau, just to name a few. But none of them really achieved the superstar status that Clarke Hinkle did in the '30s. Lewellen was a topnotch punter and a pretty fair runner, passer, and receiver. Mathys could pass and run with the best of his era. Kotal was a slashing runner and receiver. Basing could bull his way through the line. Lambeau could run and throw. All good backs.

Hinkle could do everything except pass. He could punt with anybody in the league. He was an excellent place-kicker, too. Above all, he was a power runner with speed. He could pound a line and drive back the best defenders in the league, including the legendary Bronko Nagurski. Their famous head-to-head encounters have been told and retold for decades, and hopefully, the tellings will go on forever because Hinkle and Nagurski played in time of little padding on players and no face masks on leather helmets. When they met head-to-head, they really did meet head-to-head, and often only one of them got up for the next play.

Hinkle was among the earliest inductees into the NFL Hall of Fame as well as the Packer Hall of Fame. His contribution to the game can't be measured in yards and touchdowns. Only the fading echoes of crunching tackles and devastating blocks, only the long vanished trail of crumpled tacklers and breathless ball carriers that he left behind can attest Hinkle's worth as a consummate player of his day and all days since.

37. What college did Hinkle attend?

38. What position did Hinkle play on offense?

39. What position did Hinkle play on defense?

40. When he retired from the Packers, what records did Hinkle hold?

41. When was Hinkle inducted into the Pro Football Hall of Fame?

42. When was Hinkle inducted into the Packer Hall of Fame?

43. How many years did Hinkle play for the Packers?

44. How many times was Hinkle selected to the All-Pro team?

Don Hutson.

Just about everything that can be written about Don Hutson in a book like this is in the **FACTS** section.

For this space, little can be added except to state that Don Hutson was the greatest receiver of all time, even better than Jerry Rice and Sterling Sharpe when one considers the differences in how the game was played in Hutson's time and how it is played now. Consider the number of games per season, consider the number of plays teams run now as opposed to the number run in Hutson's day, consider the number of passes thrown in a modern game as opposed to the inconsistency of the Packers' passing game under Curly Lambeau.

Not until 1942 did a Packer passer throw the ball more than 20 times a game when Cecil Isbell threw 268 passes in 11 games, completing 146. Those attempts and completions averaged out to 24 and 13 per game. Hutson caught 74 passes that year for an average of 6.7 per game. Don Majkowski threw 599 times and completed 343 passes in 1989 in 16 games for averages of 37 attempts and 22 completions per game. If Isbell had thrown the ball 37 times a game with his completion rate and not Majkowski's, he would have completed 220 passes. How many would Hutson have caught? How about 111 in only 11 games? Stretch that out over 16 games and he would have caught 162 passes in one season. Kind of makes Sharpe's record of 112 pale in comparison, doesn't it?

Don Hutson was the greatest receiver of all time. Enough said.

45. What college did Hutson attend?

46. What position did Hutson play on offense?

47. What position did Hutson play on defense?

48. When he retired from the Packers, what records did Hutson hold?

49. When was Hutson inducted into the Pro Football Hall of Fame?

50. When was Hutson inducted into the Packer Hall of Fame?

51. How many years did Hutson play for the Packers?

52. How many times was Hutson selected to the All-Pro team?

7
THE FALL OF CURLY LAMBEAU

The War Between the Leagues.

World War II ended before the start of the '45 football season, and some of the players who had gone off to fight for their country returned home in time to play for their team. It was the last peace they would know until a brief respite from hostilities in 1950.

During the last years of the war, several entrepreneurs tried to form leagues to compete with the NFL. Two of these would-be circuits never played a single game. A third played part of a season, and the fourth nearly bankrupted itself and the NFL in a war that lasted four years before a merger brought on peace.

1. What were the names of the two paper leagues that never played a single game?

2. What famous former football player was hired to be president of one of those leagues?

3. What was the name of the league that got off the ground but crashed half way through its only season?

4. What was the name of the league that mounted a successful challenge against the NFL?

5. What former Green Bay resident and Notre Dame player was chosen to be the first president of the new league that succeeded against the NFL?

6. What year did the new league begin play?

7. How many teams played in the new league in its first year?

8. Which franchise folded after only one season in the new league?

9. What was the name of the franchise that joined the new league for its second season?

10. Which team changed its nickname for the new league's second season?

11. Which two franchises merged for the league's final season?

12. Which team changed its nickname for the new league's final season?

13. Which three franchises of the new league became members of the NFL

in 1950?

Farewell, Curly!

The Cleveland Rams won the NFL Western Division title and the NFL crown in 1945, becoming the first team in 10 years to break the stranglehold the Bears and Packers had on the division and the "Big Four"—the Bears, Packers, Giants, and Redskins—had on the NFL.

The Packers finished third that year, their lowest resting place since ending up third in 1934. The next two years they clawed their way to third place finishes, but they would not mount a challenge for the division crown again until 1959.

Green Bay had some positives over the other members of the NFL, but it also had some heavy negatives. On the plus side, the Packers paid no executives to run the organization; the president, other officers, and board members worked for free; this was a big cost savings. In the debit column, the Packers had the smallest stadium in the NFL and the lowest attendance; revenue was much lower than other teams.

As long as the NFL had no serious competition for players, the Packers could get away with paying low salaries to their players. Halas did it in Chicago, Marshall in Washington, and Mara in New York. The NFL had a virtual, if not actual, monopoly on playing talent. The new league changed all that when its owners hired away several established players and even more college players with bigger salaries, giving the average player $500 a game and the stars over $1,000 a game. The Packers couldn't afford to pay out money like that. If the merger hadn't come when it did, the Packers would have been forced to move or to fold.

Throughout this period, Curly Lambeau and a few associates plotted to regain the franchise and move it. Fortunately, they were foiled, and the Packers remain in Green Bay to this day.

15. What was the name of the only player that the Packers lost to the new league at the beginning of the '46 season?

16. What was the name of the minor league team that had a working

contract with the Packers in 1946?

17. What was the name of the training facility that the Packers purchased in 1946?

18. Who was the Packers' first round draft choice in 1946?

19. Where did the other NFL moguls want to move the Packers for the '46 season?

20. Which former Packer's speech about a lack of support within the community started rumors that the Packers would be moving to some big city?

21. Who was the Packers' first round draft pick in 1947?

22. Who was the passer that the Packers received in a trade before the '47 season?

23. What event shocked all Packerdom in the spring of 1947?

24. What event shocked all Packerdom in the summer of 1947?

25. What team defeated the Packers for the very first time in their history in 1947?

26. Which team in the new league was rumored to be negotiating with Lambeau for his coaching services after the '47 season?

27. Who stopped Lambeau from leaving the Packers for another team after the '47 season?

28. Who was the Packers' first round draft choice in 1948?

29. Which Packer draftee was named Most Outstanding Player for the College All-Stars in the '48 game with the NFL champion Chicago Cardinals?

30. What was the new mark for futility that the Packers set in 1948?

31. What infamous distinction did the '49 Packers achieve?

32. What tragedy turned out to be a blessing for the Packers in 1950?

33. Which three directors voted against renewing Lambeau's coaching contract at the end of the '49 season?

34. Who was Lambeau's number one accomplice in his attempt to regain the Green Bay franchise as his personal property?

35. Who is most responsible for stopping Lambeau from taking the franchise away from the corporation?

36. When did Lambeau resign from the Packers and thus end an era in Green Bay history?

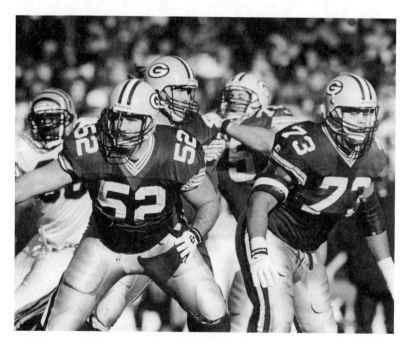

FRANK WINTERS (52) and AARON TAYLOR (73) set up to pass-block for Brett Favre.

GEORGE KOONCE

PACKER
THIS
'N'
DATA

EDGAR BENNETT

1
FIRSTS

The Packers, like any other professional team and organization, have had a lot of "firsts" in their history. Some of them are rather significant; others not. These are some of both.

1. Who was the Packers' first coach (1919 town team)?

2. Who was the Packers' first coach in the NFL?

3. Who was the Packers' first quarterback (1919 town team)?

4. Who was the Packers' first quarterback in the NFL?

5. Who was the Packers' first full-time scout?

6. Who was the first radio announcer on commercial broadcasts of Packer games?

7. Who were the first live, on-the-scene radio announcers of Packer games?

8. Which team was the Packers' first NFL opponent?

9. Which team was the first NFL team that the Packers defeated?

10. Where did the Packers play their first home game (1919 town team)?

11. Where did the Packers play their first NFL home game?

12. Which team was the Packers first NFL road opponent?

13. When did the Packers first play the Chicago Bears? (Trick question.)

14. When did the Packers first play the New York Giants?

15. When did the Packers beat the Bears for the very first time?

16. When did the Packers win their first NFL title? (This should be an easy one. The stock market crashed the same year, and something was in the news about the devil needing long underwear.)

17. When did the Packers suffer their first losing season?

18. When did the Packers win their first division title?

19. When did the Packers win their first post-season game? (Another trick question.)

20. Who was the Packers' first ever college draft pick?

21. When did the Packers play their first ever playoff game?

22. When did the Packers finish in last place for the first time?

23. When did the Packer band first play at home games?

24. Who was the first president of the Packer corporation?

25. When were the Packers' first involved in a regular season overtime game?

26. When did the Packers first defeat the Minnesota Vikings?

27. When did the Packers first defeat the Tampa Bay Buccaneers?

28. Last trick question for this section. When did the Packers first defeat the Detroit Lions?

29. When did the Packers first defeat the Jacksonville Jaguars?

30. When did the Packers first defeat the Baltimore Ravens?

2
POST-SEASON PLAY

Early Playoffs.

Playoffs as they are known today did not come into existence until the completion of the merger of the American Football League into the National Football League in 1970. Prior to that, the NFL began playoffs between its four division winners in 1967 to determine the team that would appear in the Super Bowl, and the AFL added a tier of playoffs in 1969.

The Packers became involved in playoff games long before any of this. In fact, they played in the very first playoff game in NFL history. Since then, they have appeared in eight more games on the road to an NFL title.

1. When did the Packers first appear in a playoff game?

2. What was the result of that first playoff game?

3. Who did the Packers defeat for the Western Conference title in 1965?

4. Who did the Packers defeat in the '66 NFL playoff game, putting Green Bay into the first Super Bowl?

5. After the Packers won the Central Division in 1967, which team did they defeat in the first round of the NFL playoffs?

The Ice Bowl.

The most famous game in Packer history is the fabled "Ice Bowl" of 1967. How much do you know about this NFL championship game?

6. What was the date of the game?

7. Who was the Packers' opponent?

8. What was the official temperature at game time?

9. Who was the Packers' coach?

10. Who was the opponents' coach?

11. Who was the opponents' quarterback?

12. Who scored the Packers' first two touchdowns?

13. Who scored the Packers' final touchdown?

14. What was the final score?

15. What was the official attendance?

16. What was the unofficial attendance?

Playoffs Since the Merger of the NFL and AFL.

Life hasn't been all that great for the Packers since the AFL and the NFL became the AFC and NFC in the NFL in 1970. Thru 1993, they have made the Playoffs only three times. Not much to brag about here, but there were some moments.

17. Who was the Packers' coach when they played the Washington Redskins in the first round of the '72 Playoffs?

18. Who was the Packers' coach when they next made the Playoffs?

19. What was unusual about the year the Packers' made the Playoffs in the previous question?

20. What were the Playoffs called that year?

21. What team did the Packers play in Green Bay in those Playoffs?

22. What team eliminated the Packers that year?

23. What team did the Packers defeat in the first round of the '93 Playoffs?

24. What team eliminated the Packers in the '93 Playoffs, the '94 Playoffs, and the '95 Playoffs?

25. What team did the Packers defeat in the first round of the '94 Playoffs?

26. What team did the Packers defeat in the first round of the '95 Playoffs?

27. How many times had the Packers played the San Francisco 49ers in the Playoffs before they beat the defending Super Bowl champions in the second round of the '95 Playoffs?

28. How many times have the Packers beaten the San Francisco 49ers in the Playoffs since they beat defending Super Bowl champions in the second round of the '95 Playoffs?

29. What Packer record did Lynn Dickey tie in the Packers' '83 Playoff game against St. Louis?

30. Who did the Packers defeat for the NFC championship in 1996?

31. What Packer tied a Playoff record against the Dallas Cowboys in 1983?

Championship Games.

The Packers have played in more title games than any team in the history of the NFL. That's some distinction, but even more impressive is the fact that the Packers have won more NFL titles than any other team in the league's history.

32. What team have the Packers played the most for the NFL title?

33. How many times did the Packers play the team in the previous question for the NFL title?

34. Which two teams have defeated the Packers in a championship game?

35. Which Packer coach won six NFL titles?

36. Which Packer coaches won the rest of the Packers' NFL titles?

37 What years did the Packers win NFL titles?

38. Which of the Packers' NFL title games prior to the advent of the Super Bowl was played at a neutral site?

39. Who was the Packers' opponent for that neutral site game?

40. What is the longest time period the Packers have gone without winning the NFL championship?

41. Who was the Packers' opponent in the 1938, 1939, 1944, 1961, and 1962 NFL title games?

42. Where was the '39 championship game played?

43. What was each Packer's share of the receipts of the Packers' first championship game?

44. What game resulted in the first million dollar gate receipts in NFL history?

Super Bowls.
Every good Packer fan and even some Bear fans know that the Packers won the first two Super Bowls and Super Bowl XXXI. But how much do you know about those three historic games?

45. What was the site of Super Bowl I?

46. What was the final score of Super Bowl I?

47. Who was the Packers' opponent in Super Bowl II?

48. What was the final score of Super Bowl II?

49. What was the winning player's share of the first Super Bowl?

50. Who did the Packers face in Super Bowl XXXI?

51. Where was Super Bowl XXXI played?

52. What was the final score of Super Bowl XXXI?

53. Who was voted Most Valuable Player for Super Bowl XXXI?

54. Who was voted Most Valuable Player for Super Bowl I?

55. Who was voted Most Valuable Player in Super Bowl II?

56. The Packers as a team set one record in Super Bowl XXXI, but it was actually set by one man. What record was this?

The Playoff Bowl.
The what? This is real trivia. Who can remember the Playoff Bowl? You get points just for knowing what it was.

What it was: The geniuses who ran the NFL in the '50s and '60s thought the fans would buy an extra game on the season that meant nothing whatsoever, just like a majority of the college bowl games. So they invented the Playoff Bowl where the second place teams in the two NFL conferences would play at a neutral site. There was nothing at stake except pride and the right to say your team was the third best in the NFL that year.

57. How many times did the Packers play in the Playoff Bowl?

58. How many times did the Packers win the Playoff Bowl?

59. How many times did the Packers lose the Playoff Bowl?

60. How many fans cared about the Playoff Bowl?

3
GREEN BAY VS. CHICAGO

Before the Bears and Cardinals.

When Packer fans think of Chicago, their blood pressure rises as images of the navy blue uniforms of the hated Chicago Bears come to mind. This distaste for Chicago's only current team began in 1919 when George Whitney Calhoun wrote about the Packers facing a big city eleven from the Windy City.

1. What was the first Chicago team that the Packers played?

2. What was the name of the semi-pro team that the Packers played two consecutive years?

3. What was the name of the other Chicago athletic club that the Packers played before beginning their league slate in 1921?

4. What Illinois city was the official home of the Staleys before they moved officially to Chicago in 1921?

5. Who was the famous player-coach of the Chicago Staleys?

The Chicago Cardinals.

The Cardinals (now the Arizona Cardinals) started out as an athletic club in Chicago in the 19th Century. They were a charter member of the NFL (nee APFA) in 1920, moved to St. Louis in 1960, then moved to Arizona in 1988. While in Chicago, the Cardinals were surpassed in futility only by the Pittsburgh Steelers. Since leaving Chicago, the Cardinals have been the masters of mediocrity.

6. Who was the founder of the Cardinals?

7. What was the name of the athletic club that became known as the

Cardinals?

8. How did the Cardinals get their nickname?

9. Before they became known as the Cardinals, what was the team's nickname?

10. When did the Packers first play the Cardinals in an NFL regular season game?

11. When did the Packers first defeat the Cardinals in an NFL regular season game?

12. Which NFL team was the first to play the Cardinals at Comiskey Park?

13. What was unique about the scheduling of games between the Packers and Cardinals in the '30s?

14. What the unique feature of the Packers-Cardinals series in 1938?

15. During World War II, when the NFL was faced with a shortage of players, the Cardinals merged with another NFL team for one season. Which team was it?

16. In what year did the Packers contribute two losses to the Cardinals' drive to the NFL title?

17. What former Packer quarterback coached the Cardinals to their first title in 1925?

18. What former Packer coach served in the same capacity with the Cardinals for one full season and 10 games of another?

19. Who was the Hall-of-Famer to coach the Cardinals in their first season in the NFL?

20. What was the name of the Cardinals' owner who died just months before his team won their first title in over 20 years?

Duh Bears!

The Chicago Bears were officially born January 28, 1922, when George Halas and his partner Ed Sternaman were granted a franchise in the NFL. Some historians have assumed that the franchise owned by A.E. Staley of the Staley Starch Company had been transferred to Halas and Sternaman; thus, it had continuity from one owner to another.

This was not true.

Halas and Sternaman had a rival for the Staley franchise —one Bill Harley, brother of Chick Harley who had played for Halas the year before. Staley gave the franchise document—the one that granted him the right to field a team from Decatur, Illinois, in the league —to Halas to take to the league meeting where Halas was supposed to have it transferred into his and Sternaman's names—without a hitch. Halas followed his instructions, adding that he wanted it granted to them for the city of Chicago. Before the league officials could make the transfer, the Harley brothers let it be known that they had been promised a franchise for the city of Chicago by Halas in exchange for Chick's services as a player.

Joe Carr, league president and owner of the Columbus (Ohio) franchise, and the other owners—Halas not included—voted to listen to both sides, heard them out, then called Staley back in Decatur. Staley chose not to be dragged into the argument between the Harleys and Halas and Sternaman. Instead, he informed Carr that he was turning in the franchise for Decatur, and the league could do as it wished concerning the Harleys and Halas.

Carr and the owners voted to accept the return of Staley's franchise, but they chose not to give it Halas and Sternaman as Staley had requested. Instead, they entertained applications from both parties for a franchise for Chicago. Halas and Sternaman won out, and the Harleys were granted a franchise for Toledo as a consolation.

Proof of all this the fact that Halas and Sternaman were granted a franchise to be known as the Chicago Bears. Check the records.

21. When were the Packers first scheduled to play the Bears?

22. When was the first game between the Bears and Packers in Chicago?

23. When was the first time the Packers beat the Bears in Chicago?

24. When was the first time the Packers beat the Bears twice in one season?

25. When was the first time the Packers beat the Bears three times in one season?

26. When was the first time the Packers lost to the Bears twice in one season?

27. When was the only time the Packers lost three times to the Bears in one season?

28. When was the only year the Packers played the Bears in Milwaukee in a regular season game?

29. What is the longest winning streak the Packers have ever had over the Bears?

30. What is the longest losing streak the Packers have ever had against the Bears?

31. How many consecutive years did the Packers and Bears play each other before the string was broken?

32. How many consecutive years did the Packers and Bears meet in the Shrine Game, starting in 1959?

33. How many times have the Packers and Bears gone into overtime?

34. When did Chester Marcol score his only touchdown in the NFL?

35. Which Packer coach never beat the Bears?

36. How many times have the Packers beaten the Bears with Brett Favre as their starting quarterback?

37. What is the Packers' record against the Bears in games played on Halloween?

4
OTHER OPPONENTS

Non-NFL Opposition.

The Packers have played over 100 different teams since 1919. Before the advent of the pro league, the Packers' opponents were town teams and athletic clubs. Even after joining the NFL, they continued to play non-league teams as warmups for the championship season and as money-raisers during the season. Some of these pro and semi-pro squads weren't too bad; however, most were merely fodder for the bullies from Green Bay.

1. What was the only team to beat the Packers in both of the two seasons before they joined the NFL?

2. What Illinois pro team did the Packers play prior to the 1921 season?

3. What pro team did the Packers play at the end of the 1921 season for the mythical Wisconsin state championship?

4. What pro team did the Packers play before the beginning of the 1922 season and on Thanksgiving Day that year?

5. What Minnesota pro team did the Packers host before the 1923 season?

6. What Upper Peninsula team did the Packers play three years running as a pre-season tuneup?

7. What former NFL team did the Packers play before the 1928 season?

8. What future NFL team did the Packers play before the 1929 season?

9. What town team was supplemented by college players to play the Packers before the 1934 season?

10. What four Wisconsin town teams did the Packers play before the 1935 campaign?

NFL Opponents.

The NFL has had a lot of teams over the years. Some franchises, such as the Cardinals and the Colts, have played in several cities during their histories. The Packers haven't played them all, but they have played an awful lot of those teams.

11. What city was the home of the Crimson Giants?

12. What city was the home of the Panhandles?

13. What was the nickname of the Kansas City team that the Packers dumped twice in 1924?

14. What 1925 Packers' victim had a presidential nickname?

15. What one-time NFL champion never beat the Packers and folded in the middle of the Great Depression?

16. What was the "neighborhood" team that sat out the '32 campaign but came back into the NFL in 1933 with a new name and a new owner?

17. What was the original nickname of the Pittsburgh Steelers?

18. What was the nickname of the first Detroit team to play the Packers?

19. What were the nicknames of the teams that called Brooklyn home?

20. What was the Packers' record against the Brooklyn teams?

21. What city did the Rams call home before Los Angeles and St. Louis?

22. What do the Boston Yanks, Cleveland Bulldogs, Cleveland Indians,

Cincinnati Reds, Dallas Texans, Dayton Triangles, Hammond Pros, Louisville Colonels, Minneapolis Marines, Minneapolis Red Jackets, New York Bulldogs, Racine Tornadoes, and St. Louis Gunners have in common?

23. Since the Cardinals moved to Arizona, how many time have they defeated the Packers?

24. Which is the only old AFL team that the Packers have a winning record over?

25. How many teams have represented New York City against the Packers in the NFL? Brooklyn and Staten Island don't count.

26. How many times have expansion teams defeated the Packers in their first NFL seasons?

27. How many times have the Rams beaten the Packers since moving to St. Louis?

28. How many teams from Dallas have the Packers played over the years?

29. How many states have the Packers played regular season games in?

30. Which city has had the most teams that have played the Packers?

31. Which old AFL team have the Packers never beaten?

32. Since the Colts moved to Indianapolis, what is the Packers' record against them?

33. Since the Browns (now the Ravens) were switched to the AFC in 1970, what is the Packers' record against them?

34. How many times have the Packers beaten the Steelers since they were shifted to the AFC in 1970?

The Black and Blue Rivalry.

The Packers have played in the Western Conference, the Western

Division, the NFL Central Division, and the NFC Central Division. The two constants in all those divisions and conferences were the Chicago Bears and Detroit Lions. Since 1961, the Minnesota Vikings have become part of that group, and the Tampa Bay Bucs joined up in 1977. The Packers and Bears began mauling each other back in the 1920s, and the Lions (nee Portsmouth Spartans) dealt out their own brand of punishment to the two senior teams in 1930. The Vikings realized early on, that if they were ever to be winners in the division, then they would have to bang heads with the big guys in the same fashion. The Bucs learned that lesson when they came into the league.

The battles between the Packers and Bears have been chronicled by Glenn Swain in his book, *Packers vs. Bears*, and by Gary D'Amato and Cliff Christl in their book, *Bloodbaths and Mudbaths*. But the overall rivalry between all five teams in the current NFC Central Division is best detailed in a new book by noted author and radio personality Wayne Mausser in his book, *The Black and Blue Rivalry*.

35. If one man is responsible for lighting the fire of bitter competition between the Bears and the Packers, who would he be?

36. Who was the head coach of the Portsmouth Spartans when they entered the NFL in 1930?

37. When the Spartans were moved to Detroit, who was their head coach?

38. What year did the Lions win the division championship for the first time?

39. What decade did the Lions have their so-called dynasty?

40 . What year did the NFL put the Lions, Bears, Packers, and Vikings in a single division?

41. Who was the first head coach of the Minnesota Vikings?

42. Who was the first head coach of the Tampa Bay Bucs?

43. Since the formation of the Central Division, which team has won the most division titles?

44. Who was the head coach of the Vikings when they won their first Central Division crown?

45. What year did the Tampa Bay Bucs win the Central Division for the first time?

46. Which Chicago head coach had the most success in the Central Division since its inception?

47. Since the merger of the NFL and AFL, the Packers have played every team in their division twice in all but one year. What year was it?

48. The Central Division holds a distinction that no other division in the NFL has. What is it? Hint: It involves post-season play.

49. How many times has a Central Division team represented the NFC in the Super Bowl?

50. How many Super Bowls have NFC Central Division teams won?

5
STADIUMS
AND OTHER FACILITIES

The Packers have played in several different homes over the years. They've played on fields marked off in local parks, fields without fences to control the crowds, baseball stadia, and one of the finest football arenas in the history of the game: Lambeau Field.

Besides their regular season playgrounds, the Packers have had some rather interesting practice fields. At one time, they practiced in a vacant lot in downtown Green Bay; the newspaper building was next door. They even practiced at a brewery one year. Now they have the best indoor practice field in the NFL. What does this say about the Packers and the people of Green Bay?

1. The Packers' first home playing field was named after what?

2. What was the name of the baseball park the Packers used in 1923 and 1924 as their home field?

3. What year was old City Stadium first used by the Packers?

4. What was the original name of Lambeau Field?

5. What prominent American politician came to Green Bay for the dedication of the new stadium?

6. What was the original capacity of Lambeau Field?

7. What is the current capacity of Lambeau Field to the nearest thousand?

8. When the executive committee first decided to expand Lambeau Field, who said the following? "You'll never fill it."

9. When was the present Packer Hall of Fame dedicated?

10. What prominent American was present for the dedication of the packer Hall of Fame?

11. What were the names of the two stadiums that the Packers used in the Milwaukee area prior to Milwaukee County Stadium?

12. What was the capacity of Milwaukee County Stadium when used for football to the nearest thousand?

13. What was Rockwood Lodge?

14. What was the cost, to the nearest $100,000, of Lambeau Field when it was first built?

15. What year were the first skyboxes added to Lambeau Field?

16. When was the Hutson Center built?

6
THE MEDIA

1. What was the first year in which all Packer games were televised?

2. What were the call letters and locations of the two radio stations over which a number of Packer games were broadcast in 1941?

3. In what year was the Green Bay Packer Yearbook first published?

4. Who was the radio voice of the Packers from 1952 thru 1956?

5. What former Packer player was the color commentator on the '85 Packer radio broadcasts?

6. Who was the Packer television announcer from 1956 thru 1965?

7. What former color commentator on Packer television broadcasts has been both a Packer player and a Packer executive?

8. Who was the radio voice of the Packers in 1986?

9. What was the name of the Green Bay *Press-Gazette* editor who helped organize the Packers and was the first Packer publicity director?

10. What former Packer founded a Packer oriented newspaper?

11. What former newspaper reporter became the publicity director for the Packers?

12. What former newspaper sports editor became a columnist for *The Packer Report* and editor emeritus for *The Packer Yearbook*?

13. Who joined the radio broadcast team for the Packer Radio Network as

a color commentator in 1995?

14. What NFL Hall of Famer did the color analysis on Packer pre-season games that were telecast in Wisconsin only, originating from a station Green Bay?

15. Who did the play-by-play announcing for Channel 2 in Green Bay when that station telecast pre-season games in the 1980s and 1990s?

7
WHO IS HE?

In each of the following questions, five hints are given about the identity of the person being described.

1. He was on the Packers' active roster in 1956 and 1958-1970. He played his college football at SMU. He played for the Dallas Cowboys after leaving the Packers. During his last few seasons on the active Packers' roster, he was a player-coach. He coached the Cincinnati Bengals to the '82 Super Bowl. Who is he?

2. He had 79 career interceptions. He was a defensive back for the Packers from 1959 thru 1961. He played for the New York Giants from 1948 thru 1958. He is a member of the Pro Football Hall of Fame. His initials are the same as the title of a popular movie of the early '80s. Who is he?

3. He led the NFL in scoring in 1938. He was inducted in the Pro Football Hall of Fame in 1964. He led the NFL in field goals in 1940 and 1941. He played his college football at Bucknell. He was a runner, a defensive back, a passer, a place kicker, and a punter. Who is he?

4. He led the NFL in field goals in 1943. He played his college football at Alabama. He is a charter member of the Pro Football Hall of Fame. He led the NFL for eight years in receiving. He holds the Packer record for the most touchdowns scored in a career. Who is he?

5. He once completed 35 passes in a game (a Packer record). He once held the Packer season records for the most pass attempts, most passes completed, most yards gained passing, and most TD passes. He played his college football at Kansas State. He was obtained by the Packers in a trade with the Houston Oilers. He had more professional football experience than anyone else on the '85 Packers' roster. Who is he?

6. As a blocking back/linebacker, he was considered the top Packer rookie of 1933. He played on three Packer championship teams. He played his college football at Wisconsin. He is best remembered as a Packer guard. After retiring from football, he operated a restaurant in the Milwaukee area for many years. Who is he?

7. He played his college football under Knute Rockne. He was known primarily as a running back as a Packer player, although he played other positions including safety on defense. He is a charter member of the Pro Football Hall of Fame, the Packer Hall of Fame, and is also in the Wisconsin Hall of Fame. He worked for a packing company after leaving college due to an illness. The current Green Bay football stadium is named for him. Who is he?

8. He played halfback for the Packers from 1929-33 and 1935-36. His home town was New Richmond, Wisconsin. He played his college football at St. Johns of Minnesota. He was well known for his off-the-field activities. He got his playing name from the marquee of a Rudolph Valentino movie. Who is he?

9. His professional football career, as a player and coach, lasted from 1926 thru 1956. He is a member of the Pro Football Hall of Fame. He played guard on the Packers' '36 championship team, and was a Packer coach from 1945 thru 1948. Before coming to Green Bay, he played with Duluth, Pottsville, and Chicago. After retiring as a player, he coached in Pittsburgh. Who is he?

10. He was the second Packer head coach who also played for the Packers. A tribute to him was attended by President Richard Nixon. He spent more years as a Packer quarterback than any other man in Packer history. He once provided color commentary on network television. He was the most valuable player in each of the first two Super Bowls. Who is he?

11. This Packer player made it into the NFL Hall of Fame. He went to Syracuse and was a seventh round draft choice in 1953. He was an eight-time All-Pro, seven with the Packers, and played in 10 Pro Bowls. He once held the record for playing in the most consecutive games, his mark being 183. He played on two NFL championship teams, and he finished his career in Philadelphia. Who is he?

12. This Packer player went undrafted out of college and wrote to several NFL teams asking for a tryout. Lombardi gave him one. He went to college at Southern California. He played 12 years for the Packers. He played in six NFL championship games, made All-Pro six times, and played in eight Pro Bowls. He intercepted 48 passes during his Packer career. His interception of a Len Dawson pass in Super Bowl I was turning point in the game. Who is he?

8
NICKNAMES

By what nickname was the each of the following Packer players and coaches more commonly known? Some of these are too easy, but not everything has to be difficult. Or does it?

1. Earl Girard	8. Howard Buck
2. John McNally	9. Vito Parilli
3. Ray McLean	10. Fred Thurston
4. Charles Goldenberg	11. Bernard Darling
5. Floyd Reid	12. Reggie White
6. Paul Engebretsen	13. Paul Hornung
7. Earl Lambeau	14. Larry McCarren

9
REAL NAMES

What was the real first name of each of the following Packer players and coaches? Now these are hard. Not everything has to be easy either. Good luck!

1. Bart Starr

2. Hog Hanner

3. Zeke Bratkowski

4. Jess Whittenton

5. Forrest Gregg

6. Mike Michalske

7. Max McGee

8. Liz Blackbourn

9. Cal Hubbard

10. Bill Forester

11. Sean Jones

12. Dorsey Levens

10
COLLEGE FOOTBALL

At what college or university did each of the following Packers play football?

1. Keith Wortman, Tyrone Williams, Charlie Brock, Vern Lewellen, Vince Ferragamo, Bob Kahler, Royal Kahler, Herman Rohrig, George Sauer, Jerry Tagge.

2. Al Del Greco, David Beverly, Brent Fullwood, Keith Uecker, Ed West, James Willis.

3. Red Dunn, Wayland Becker, Art Bultman, Lavvie Dilweg, Chester Johnston, Jab Murray, Whitey Woodin.

4. Roger Zatkoff, Norm Masters, Mike Jolly, John Anderson, Don Bracken, Ed Frutig, Harlan Huckleby, Ron Kramer, Bob Mann, Bo Molenda, Desmond Howard.

5. Paul Hornung, Tim Huffman, Blair Kiel, Curly Lambeau, Mike P. McCoy (DT), Red Smith, Craig Hentrich, Aaron Taylor, Derrick Mayes.

6. Don Wells, Zeke Bratkowski, Hurdis McCrary, Tom Nash, Floyd Reid, Pete Tinsley.

7. Willie Buchanan, Mike Douglass, Don Horn, Rich Moran.

8. Terry Jones, Jim Bowdoin, Scott Hunter, Don Hutson, Bill Lee, Claude Perry, Randy Scott, Bart Starr, Rich Wingo, Byron Braggs, George Teague.

9. Cub Buck, Steve Wagner, Ken Bowman, Milt Gantenbein, Milt Gardner, Jug Girard, Buckets Goldenberg, Eddie Jankowski, Champ Seibold, Ken Stills, Deral Teteak, Randy Wright.

10. Glen Sorenson, Lionel Aldridge, John Thompson, Ron Cassidy, MacArthur Lane, Carl Mulleneaux.

11. Mark Koncar, Dan Grimm, Boyd Dowler, Gary Knafelc, Mike C. McCoy (DB), Darius Holland.

12. Tony Mandarich, Herb Adderly, Hank Bullough, Frank Butler, Dan Currie, Roger Grove, Norm Masters, Bobby Monnett, Bill Quinlan.

13. Leotis Harris, Lew Carpenter, Jessie Clark, Bob Forte, Dave Hanner, Greg Koch, Bill Brown.

14. Gale Gillingham, Jim Carter, Bill Kuusisto, Eddie Glick, Carl Lidberg, Dick O'Donnell, Urban Odson, Earl Svendsen, George Svendsen, Dick Wildung.

15. Tom Bettis, Lou Brock, Cecil Isbell, Perry Williams.

16. Ezra Johnson.

17. Tiny Cahoon, Tony Canadeo, Hector Cyre.

18. Joe Johnson, Karl Swanke, Mark Chmura.

19. David Whitehurst.

20. Lou Gordon, Ray Nitschke, Jim Grabowski, Larry McCarren.

21. Guy Prather, Roderick Mullen, Patrick Scott, Willie Davis.

22. Pid Purdy, John MacAuliffe, Boob Darling, Walter McGaw, Bill DeMoe.

23. Hank Bruder, Frank Baker.

24. Billy Grimes, Derrel Gofourth.

25. Chuck Mercein.

26. Fred Cone, Larry Hefner, Wayne Simmons.

27. Jerry Kramer.

28. Bob Brown.

29. Johnny Gray.

30. Dave Robinson.

31. Cliff Lewis, Terry Wells, Brett Favre.

32. Lenny McGill, Travis Williams, John Jefferson, Scott Stephen, Craig Newsome, Shawn Patterson, Dennis Sproul, Brian Noble.

33. Alex Urban, Robert Brooks, Charley Brock, Sterling Sharpe.

34. Adam Timmerman.

35. Sean Jones.

36. Bill Stevens, Jesse Whittenton, Chris Jacke.

37. Barry Smith, Ron Lewis, Leroy Butler, Terrell Buckley, Edgar Bennett, Alphonso Carreker.

38. Veryl Switzer, Paul Coffman, Lynn Dickey.

39. Mel Jackson, Brian Williams, Bill Hayhoe, Ken Ruettgers, Lamont Hollinquest, Ernie Smith, John Michels, Willie Wood, Nate Barrager.

40. John Roach, Eddie Garcia, Val Joe Walker, Forrest Gregg, Gene Wilson, Bill Forester.

41. Allen Brown, Bill Kinard, Tony Bennett.

42. Charley Mathys, Nate Borden, John Hadl, Bob Skoronski.

43. Gilbert Brown, Harry Sydney, Mike Butler.

44. Tom Brown.

45. Mike Weddington, Jack Jacobs, Rich Turner, George Cumby, Fred Nixon, Keith Jackson.

11
PACKER RECORDS

Ball Carriers.

A lot of running backs have toted the ball for the Packers since 1921. Statistics weren't kept for those earliest runners, but starting in 1931 that changed. It's unlikely that Curly Lambeau, Vern Lewellen, or Biff Basing amassed the numbers of their successors, but it would be nice to know how they did. Maybe one day some true researcher will dig out the old newspapers and total up the numbers for posterity. Until then, those early backs will have to be left out of the records.

1. Which Packer running back was the first to gain 1,000 yards in a single season?

2. Which Packer running back holds the team record for most yards gained in a single season?

3. Which Packer running back gained 1,000 yards or more five consecutive years?

4. Which Packer running back holds the team record for most rushing attempts in a single season?

5. Which Packer running back holds the team record for most rushing touchdowns in a single season?

6. Which Packer running back holds the team record for the longest run from scrimmage?

7. Which Packer running back holds the team record for the most carries in a game?

8. Which Packer running back holds the team record for most yards gained in a game?

9. Which Packer running back holds the team record for most yards gained in a career?

10. Which Packer running back scored four touchdowns in a game three times?

Passers.
    Quarterbacks in the days before the T-formation were usually blocking backs and signal callers. They seldom ran with the ball, and they passed it even less. Halfbacks and fullbacks did the passing in

Curly Lambeau's offenses. Arnie Herber and Cecil Isbell weren't quarterbacks; they were halfbacks who passed the ball as well as ran with it.

In fact, the Packers didn't have a true quarterback—in the modern sense of the term where the QB is expected to hand the ball to running backs and throw it to receivers and run with it only out of desperation—until the 1950s. An argument could be made that Jack Jacobs was a modern quarterback, but he lined up a yard behind the center instead of under the center and ran with the ball frequently as part of designed plays. Bob Thomason was probably the first true modern quarterback to play for the Packers. Some might argue that Tobin Rote was the first true quarterback, but he was also expected to run with the ball, not just pass it and hand off those first few years of his career with the Packers.

After Rote came the *first* greatest quarterback in Packer history. Since then, all Packer quarterbacks have been measured against the accomplishments of Bart Starr.

11. Who threw the most passes in one season?

12. Who threw the most passes in one game?

13. Who completed the most passes in one season?

14. Who completed the most passes in one game?

15. Although Brett Favre had 24 passes in 1993, he doesn't hold the record for most passes intercepted in one season. Who does hold the record?

16. Who had the most passes intercepted ion one game? (If you get this one right, you're a great Packer fan or you're an old Packer fan.)

17. Who threw the most touchdown passes in one season?

18. Who gained the most yards passing in one season?

19. Who threw the most touchdown passes in one game?

20. Who holds all the positive career passing records for the Packers? (This one is so easy that the answer isn't even in the answer section.)

Receivers.
Three of the greatest pass catchers in the history of the NFL have worn Packer uniforms: Don Hutson, James Lofton, and Sterling Sharpe. In due time, the name of Robert Brooks might be added to this list.

Hutson had incredible numbers during his career that have withstood the test of time.

If Lofton had played his entire career in Green Bay, who knows how high his career totals might have gone in the Packer record books?

And what if Sharpe hadn't suffered that injury to his neck? Of course, if he hadn't, Packer fans wouldn't have found out what sort of person he really was and Brooks wouldn't have gotten the opportunity to show the fans that he's everything that Sharpe was on the field and more off the field.

Let us not forget that Boyd Dowler, Billy Howton, and Max McGee also wore Packer uniforms, and none of them ever embarrassed Green Bay on the field. Although Johnny Blood doesn't have the numbers, his contemporaries called him the greatest receiver of his time. Bob Mann was a capable receiver, and out of the backfield, few can match Gerry Ellis and now Edgar Bennett.

21. Which career record does James Lofton hold for the Packers?

22. Which records does Don Hutson still hold for the Packers?

23. Which records does Sterling Sharpe hold for the Packers?

24. Who holds the record for most yards gained catching passes in one game?

25. Who caught the longest pass in Packer history?

26. Who holds the record for most yards gained catching passes in one season?

Defenders.

27. Who holds the Packer record for the longest return of an intercepted pass?

28. Who holds the Packer record for blocking the most kicks in a season?

29. Who intercepted the most passes in one season?

30. Who is the career leader in pass thefts?

31. Who recovered the most opponents' fumbles in a career?

Miscellaneous Marks.

32. Who holds the Packer record for the most touchdowns via kickoff returns in a season?

33. Who holds the Packer record for the most points scored in a single game?

34. Who holds the Packer record for most field goals kicked in a single game?

35. Who is the career leader in field goals kicked in a career?

12
UNIFORM NUMBERS

Give the uniform number worn by each of the following Packer players. It is possible that a player may have worn another number at some time, for example in his first season. However, the answers should be the numbers worn throughout most of the players' careers.

1. Eric Torkelson

2. Jim Taylor

3. Herb Adderley

4. Johnnie Gray

5. Boyd Dowler

6. Gary Knafelc

7. Dave Robinson

8. Henry Jordan

9. Don Horn

10. Jerry Kramer

11. What four Packer players have had their uniform numbers retired by the Packers?

12. Jim Ringo

13. Hank Gremminger

14. Willie Davis

15. Donny Anderson

16. Carroll Dale

17. Gale Gillingham

18. Lionel Aldridge

19. Estus Hood

20. Ron Kramer

21. Don Chandler

22. What were the numbers worn by each of the players whose numbers have been retired by the Packers?

23. Gerry Ellis

24. Brian Noble

25. Ken Ruettgers

26. What number does the statue outside the Packer Hall of Fame have?

13
WHAT POSITION DID THEY PLAY?

At what position is each of the following listed on the all-time roster?

1. Bob Hyland

2. Willie Wood

3. Larry Craig

4. David Beverly

5. Fred Cone

6. Mike Douglass

7. Greg Koch

8. Milt Gantenbein

9. Don Chandler

10. Russ Letlow

11. Dennis Claridge

12. Chester Marcol

13. Ray Stachowicz

14. Jim Ringo

15. Scott Hunter

16. Doug Evans

17. Nate Abrams

18. Barty Smith

19. Jim Carter

20. Hank Bullough

14
TRADES AND DRAFT CHOICES

1. For whom did the Packers trade Donny Anderson?

2. What did the Packers give up to acquire John Hadl from the Los Angeles Rams in 1974?

3. Who was the Packers' first round draft choice in 1982?

4. To what team was Ron Kramer traded? When?

5. From what team was John Jefferson acquired?

6. In addition to draft choices, what two players did the Packers give up for Lynn Dickey?

7. What Packer quarterback was traded to Cleveland and later reacquired by the Packers?

8. Who was the Packers' bonus pick in the '57 draft?

9. Who was their regular first round draft choice in 1957?

10. In what round was Bart Starr drafted by the Packers?

11. With what league did the Packers' 1980 first draft choice sign his first professional contract?

12. In what years did the Packers have the first draft choice of the entire NFL?

13. What two defensive ends were obtained by the Packers in the first round of the '77 draft?

14. Who was the Packers' top college draft choice in 1985?

15. What player (in addition to draft choices) was given up in the trade for John Jefferson?

16. How were Larry McCarren, Greg Boyd, and Gerry Ellis acquired by the Packers?

17. Was Jan Stenerud acquired by trade, draft, or some other method?

18. Who were the Packers' first round draft picks in 1978 and 1979?

19. From what teams were Zeke Bratkowski, Lew Carpenter, and MacArthur Lane acquired?

20. To what teams were Bill Howton and Jim Ringo traded?

21. Before Paul Hornung retired, he had been acquired by what team in the expansion draft?

22. In what year was the college draft first begun by the NFL?

23. Who was the Packers top draft choice in 1992?

24. In what round was Mark Chmura drafted?

25. In what round was Robert Brooks drafted?

26. Place-kickers aren't often drafted, but Chris Jacke was. In which round did the Packers select him?

27. Some of the best players come out of small colleges. Adam Timmerman is an example of that, coming from little South Dakota State. In which round did the Packers pick him?

15
QUARTERBACKS

1. What quarterback was the Packers' first round draft choice in 1981?

2. What quarterback was obtained in a trade with the Chicago Cardinals in 1959?

3. Four Packer quarterbacks have thrown five touchdown passes in a game. Name three of the four.

4. What quarterback helped win a championship for Detroit after being traded from the Packers?

5. What quarterback was the Packers' first round draft choice in 1952?

6. What Packer quarterback led the NFL in passing in 1962, 1964, and 1966?

7. What Packer quarterback was the leading passer in the NFL in 1941?

8. What former Wisconsin quarterback was a Packer draft choice in 1984?

9. What quarterback played for Green Bay West High School and the University of Nebraska before playing with the Packers?

10. What quarterback was involved in a trade that got Dan Devine in trouble with fans, the media, and the Packer board of directors?

11. Brett Favre started his career with the Packers as a backup quarterback to Don Majkowski. The next year Majkowski was gone. Who was Farve's primary backup from 1993-95?

16
PRO FOOTBALL HALL OF FAME

1. Where is the Pro Football Hall of Fame located?

2. What year were the charter members inducted into the Hall of Fame?

3. Name four former Packers who were selected as charter members of the Hall of Fame.

4. Name 10 of 20 additional former Packer players who have been inducted into the Hall of Fame?

5. Name the four Packer head coaches who are in the Hall of Fame.

6. Of the 20 players and coaches who represented the Packers at one time or another during their careers in the NFL, which one spent the least amount of time in Green Bay?

17
POTPOURRI

1. Who was the Packers' top draft choice in 1984?

2. What position did Milbourn Croft play for the Packers?

3. Where did Bart Starr play his college football?

4. Why did Paul Hornung miss the '63 season?

5. From what team was Don McIlhenny obtained?

6. Where did Howie Ferguson play his college football?

7. What was Baby Ray's real first name?

8. What former Packer served in the U.S. Congress?

9. Where did Harlan Huckleby play his college football?

10. What position did Jack Jacobs play for the Packers?

11. What two players share the Packer record for the most interceptions caught in one game?

12. What was Jug Earpe's real name?

13. Where did Cecil Isbell play his college football?

14. What position did Barty Smith play for the Packers?

15. What former Packer defender had sight in only one eye?

16. Name the three Packers who played the '61 season while in active military service.

17. What Packer rookie led the NFL in punt returns in 1954?

18. Who were the Packers' top two draft choices in 1986?

19. Who wrote the following books?
    Instant Replay
    Mean on Sunday
    Football and the Single Man
    This Day in Green Bay Packers History

Vince
Packers Vs. Bears

20. In what sport did Jan Stenerud receive an athletic scholarship at Montana State?

21. Who was the Packer who returned the opening kickoff against Seattle in 1978 for a touchdown and presented the ball to a hospitalized child?

18
HEAD COACHES

1. What Packer coach is credited with the first use of what later became known as the "shotgun" formation?

2. At what college or university did Lisle Blackbourn coach immediately before becoming the head coach of the Packers?

3. Which Packer head coaches were previously assistant coaches on the Packer coaching staff?

4. After Lambeau, all except one Packer head coach were chosen by the vote of the executive committee. Who was the exception?

5. What unusual event happened to Dan Devine in his first game as a coach in the NFL?

6. Who was the only Packer coach and/or general manager to have a vote on the Packer board?

7. Under what coach did the Packers have their worst season record?

8. Who acted as head coach in the last two games of the '53 Packer season?

9. What former Packer player was later a player-coach for Pittsburgh

from 1937 thru 1939?

10. Under what coach did the Packers have their best season record?

11. For how many years did Lambeau coach the Packers?

12. Under what Packer head coaches was Scooter McLean an assistant coach?

13. For what university or college did Dan Devine coach immediately before becoming the head coach of the Packers? Immediately after leaving?

14. What two former Packer head coaches later were head coaches of the Washington Redskins?

15. For what professional team did Gene Ronzani play?

16. Who was Dan Devine's quarterback coach in 1972?

17. On what dates was Bart Starr hired and fired as head coach of the Packers?

18. After whom is the Super Bowl trophy named?

19
VINCE LOMBARDI

1. For how many years did Lombardi coach the Packers?

2. Where did Lombardi play his college football?

3. Where was Lombardi's only head coaching job before becoming head coach of the Packers?

4. What was the Packers' overall league record under Lombardi?

5. Immediately before coming to the Packers, with what team was Lombardi an assistant coach?

6. What was the Packers' record in Lombardi's first season?

7. Who were the men in the offensive backfield when the Packers opened their first league season under Lombardi?

8. In what year did the Packers have their best record under Lombardi?

9. How many NFL championships did the Packers win during Lombardi's tenure as head coach?

10. What is the lowest the Packers ever finished in their division under Lombardi?

20
PACKER PERSONNEL

Indicate what connection each of the following has had with the Packer organization.

1. Bud Jorgenson

2. Dad Braisher

3. Eugene Brusky

4. Wally Cruice

5. Chuck Lane

6. Jim Coffeen

7. Dominic Gentile

8. Johnny Lujack

9. Wilner Burke

10. Tony Flynn

11. John Torinus, Sr.

12. Tom Braatz

13. Andrew B. Turnbull

14. Nathan Abrams

21
STERLING SHARPE

1. What year was Sharpe drafted? In what round?

2. Which college did Sharpe attend?

3. In 1993, Sharpe broke the season pass receiving record for the Packers and the National Football League. How many passes did he catch?

4. In setting this new standard for catches in a season, Sharpe broke whose NFL record and whose Packer record?

5. Sharpe holds many pass receiving records already in his short career. Among them is most passes caught in a rookie season. Whose record did he break?

6. In 1989, Sharpe set a new record for yards gained catching passes. Whose record did he break?

7. Oddly enough, Sharpe has yet to gain 200 yards catching passes in a single game. Four other Packer receivers have done it. Name three of them.

8. Another oddity is that Sharpe has never caught more than two touchdown passes in a single game until 1993 when he tied Don Hutson for the record with four. Seven other Packer receivers have caught three touchdown passes in a game. Name five of them.

9. Sharpe set another single season record for the Packers in 1992. Name it.

10. What was the last team to prevent Sharpe from catching a pass in a regular season game?

11. Don Hutson caught 10 or more passes in a game four times in his

illustrious career. James Lofton did it twice. Thru the '94 season, how many times had Sharpe done it?

12. Sharpe has caught 50 more passes in every season as a Packer. He ranks first on the all-time Packer list. Who's second?

22
MIKE HOLMGREN

1. Holmgren is only the third Packer coach to have a winning record in his first season at the helm. Who were the other two?

2. Holmgren started his college coaching career at what California university?

3. His next coaching assignment was at Brigham Young University as quarterbacks coach in 1982. Who was his first quarterback protege that year?

4. Holmgren got a pro job in 1986 with the San Francisco 49ers. Who was his head coach?

5. Among all Packer head coaches, Holmgren holds one distinction over the rest. What is it?

6. What college did he attend?

7. What team drafted Holmgren in the eighth round of the '70 NFL Draft?

8. Holmgren coached football on the high school level in '70s, but he also coached two other sports. Name them.

9. Holmgren was hired away from the 49ers by which Packer executive?

10. While at BYU, Holmgren coached a future Packer draft choice. Name

him.

11. What does Holmgren have in common with Vince Lombardi as head coach of the Packers?

12. What is Holmgren's middle name?

23
BRETT FAVRE

Ever so often a player comes along who sparks the imaginations of fans. He brings excitement to the game with his daring play as well as with his skills. Such a player is Brett Favre.

1. What is the name of Favre's home town?

2. What is Favre's middle name?

3. Where was Favre born?

4. Where did Favre go to college?

5. What college all-star game did Favre play in and win the MVP award?

6. Which NFL team drafted Favre?

7. How many quarterbacks were drafted ahead of Favre?

8. How did the Packers obtain Favre?

9. Favre shares an NFL passing record that can never be broken. What is it?

10. What number does Favre wear?

24
REGGIE WHITE

1. Reggie was a three-sport letterman in high school. Naturally, football was one sport. What were the other two?

2. What was Reggie's hometown?

3. Where did Reggie attend college?

4. Reggie was a consensus All-American his senior year in college. He was also one of four finalists for an award given to the nation's most outstanding lineman. What was the name of this award?

5. What USFL team signed Reggie to play for them in 1984?

6. In which round was Reggie taken in NFL College Draft?

7. In his rookie year in the USFL, how many sacks did Reggie record?

8. How many years did Reggie play for the Philadelphia Eagles?

9. How many touchdowns has Reggie scored during his NFL career?

10. Which NFL quarterback has Reggie sacked the most during his career?

11. How many and in which years did Reggie lead the NFL in sacks?

12. What former NFL player claims that he had more sacks than Reggie during his career which was played mostly before sacks became an official statistic?

13. Reggie's wife performs with him in many television commercials. What is her name?

25
GUEST TRIVIA

These questions were submitted to me recently by friends and fellow Packer fans. I thought I'd share them with you.

If you have a favorite trivia question and you'd like to see it in the next edition, please submit it to the publisher at the address in the front of the book with your name, address, and a signed statement that reads: "I give my permission to Larry Names to use this question and my name, city, and state of residence in his next edition of *GREEN BAY PACKERS Facts & Trivia™*. I understand that I will not receive any monetary compensation other than a copy of the book (at a discounted price) where my question appears." Or you can use the Internet by addressing:

WWW.ATHENET.NET/~JMALECKI/PACKHIST.

Just send the same information. All names and addresses will be kept in strict confidence.

I'd be glad to include your question in the next edition which will hopefully include more Facts & Trivia™ about the Packers' participation in the Playoffs and the Super Bowl.

1. What year did Paul Hornung set the NFL record for most points scored in a season? — *Jeff Everson, Clintonville, Wis.*

2. Can you tell me who the Pack was playing and what the final score was on December 7, 1941? — *Legacy X.* (This one came across the Internet.)

3. Why, if last season (1995) was the first division title in 20 years, is Green Bay known as "Titletown"? — *Michael Harris.* (Another from the Internet.)

4. How many players who went to Notre Dame played for the Packers

before Aaron Taylor took the field in 1995? — *John Winn, Oshkosh, Wis.*

5. When was the first time the Dallas Cowboys beat the Packers? — *Tracy Ford, Roswell, N.M.*

6. How many tries did it take the Packers before they could beat the Cleveland Browns? — *Roger Gordon, North Canton, Ohio.*

7. What was the first team the Packers defeated with Vince Lombardi as head coach? — *Judi Pehler, Fond du Lac, Wis.*

8. Which NFL team was Ron Wolf's employer when the Packers hired him to be vice-president of football operations? — *Joe Malecki, Oshkosh, Wis.*

9. What is the worst beating the Packers have ever given an NFL opponent on *Monday Night Football*? — *Sue Haase, Borth, Wis.*

10. Why did Vince Lombardi end the traditional game between the Packers and the Lions in Detroit on Thanksgiving Day? — *Jim Haase, Borth Wis.*

11. Who was the Denver Broncos quarterback that made his first NFL start at Lambeau Field on December 8, 1996? — *Earl Brooker, Radio Station WVBO, Oshkosh, Wis.*

12. Who made the first quarterback sack in Super Bowl I? — *Dennis Splane, Grapevine, Texas.*

13. Who was the center for the Packers in Super Bowl I? — *Alan Deprey & Charlie Dussman, Greenacres City, Florida.*

14. What is the record attendance for any game at Lambeau Field? — *J.H. Schlaefer, Neshkoro, Wis.*

15. Of the four teams that the Packers play in the black-and-blue division, two hold winning records over the Packers. Which two? — *Wayne Mausser, Radio Station WPKR, Oshkosh, Wis., and Radio Station WPCK in Green Bay.*

16. True or false: Ben Davidson who played so many years for the Oakland Raiders and appeared in the movie *M.A.S.H.* once played for the Packers. — ***

17. Besides Bret Favre, which Packers have won the NFL's MVP award? — *Bill Ahnen, Little Suamico, Wis.*

18. Have the Packers ever had a quarterback who was a Native American? — *Joe Van Bakel*

***

Dear Readers,

Several of you sent me e-mails with trivia questions, and I asked some for permission to use your names and questions in this book. I printed out those that gave permission. Unfortunately, those letters were misplaced and have gone unfound.

If we corresponded through the Internet, please re-submit your question for the next edition.

Thank you for your patience.

— *Larry Names*

STERLING SHARPE

THE

ANSWERS

THE LAMBEAU YEARS QUIZ

1 - Before They Were Packers

1. The year was 1895.

2. The opponent was an aggregation from Stevens Point Normal school, Stevens Point, Wisconsin.

3. Final score: Stevens Point Normal 48, Green Bay 0.

4. The site of the game was Webster Avenue Park in Green Bay.

5. Marinette, Oconto, Oshkosh.

6. Green Bay lost every game. The newspapers reported only four games. So the won-lost record was 0-4.

7. Green Bay failed to score the whole season.

8. F. (Frank) Hurlbut, Jr., left end; E. Neuschwander, left tackle; J. (Joseph) Jackson, left guard; A. Hiller, center; J. (John) Gray, right guard; F. (Frank) Flatley, right tackle; B. (Bert) Banzhof, right end; A. Clements, quarterback; J. (John) Thomas, left halfback; D. (Dandy) Davis, right halfback; Fred Hulbert, fullback and captain. E. Challenger and D. Shyer, substitutes.

9. Tom Silverwood organized the second Green Bay city team.

10. Silverwood put his team on the field in 1897.

11. Tom Skenandore, a legendary athlete in the area, was hired to play for the Green Bay team.

12. The exact numbers of games isn't known, but the papers reported that the Green Bay eleven was unbeaten that year. Attesting to that

squad's accomplishments is the team photo where Tom Silverwood is holding a ball that has "Champions 1897" written over it.

13. Washington Park.

14. A Wisconsin National Guard unit, the Supply Company of the 2nd Regiment, sponsored the 1915 team.

15. Green Bay had no city team in 1916.

16. The 1916 newspapers mentioned four teams in the city league: the Hillsides Sr.; Hillsides Jr.; White City; and South Side Skiddoos.

17. The first brother to come to America was Samuel Abrahams. When he and his two brothers started receiving each other's mail, he changed his last name to Abrams and one brother changed his last name to Abrohams. The third brother kept the original spelling, Abrahams.

18. Dave Abrohams was the business manager for the 1905 team.

19. Dave Abrohams brother was Pete Abrohams, and their cousins were Isadore and Nate Abrams. All three played on city teams over the years.

20. Nate Abrams went to work at age 14 instead of finishing high school. He backed the South Side Skiddoos.

21. Nate Abrams played for the 1921 Green Bay Packers.

22. Nate Abrams organized the 1918 team.

23. The 1918 city team was nicknamed the Whales and the Bays.

24. George Whitney Calhoun managed the 1918 team.

25. Fred Hulbert.

26. Joseph Miller.

2 - The Packers Before the NFL
1. George Whitney Calhoun called the meeting for the evening of August 11, 1919.

2. Calhoun and the prospective players met in the offices of the Green Bay *Press-Gazette*.

3. The one man that Calhoun wanted to attend the first meeting didn't show up, so he called for another meeting that was held the evening of August 14, 1919.

4. No decisions were made at the first meeting. At the second meeting, Curly Lambeau showed up, and his friends voted him to be the captain of the team.

5. George Whitney Calhoun was elected to be manager of the team.

6. Lambeau and several of his teammates worked for the Indian Packing Corporation, a business that had moved to Green Bay from Providence, Rhode Island, during World War I. They convinced their

employer to supply the team with jerseys and a practice field.

7. Frank Peck's role in the beginnings of the Packers has been overlooked by many historians. Don't forget his name because if not for him the Packers may never have come into existence.

8. Calhoun called the team the Indians because of their employer, but the moniker never took hold.

9. Jim Ford, the noted TV personality who was known as "The Durkee's Olive King" because of his employer, related to this author how Calhoun told him that the nickname was originated by fellow journalist Val Schneider. John Torinus, Sr., a protégé of Calhoun, the author of *The Packer Legend* (Laranmark Press, 1982), and a famous newspaperman in Wisconsin for 50 years, told this author a different story, stating that Calhoun had told him that Emmett Platten, a Green Bay businessman who sponsored his own radio show and published a newsletter on the Packers, originated the nickname and gave it to Calhoun. I am inclined to believe the former tale because Platten's radio program and newsletter weren't begun until well after the nickname came into popular use by Calhoun and his reading public. Besides that, I came to trust Jim Ford's memory on such facts much more that John Torinus's recollections once I learned to be objective about both of these dear and close friends.

10. The Packers defeated 10 straight opponents before losing their last game of the season. Their record was 10-1.

11. The mining company teams from Ishpeming and Stambaugh were tough competition, and the Menominee squad was a traditional opponent.

12. City teams from New London, Oshkosh, Sheboygan, and Marinette were no match for the Packers of 1919.

13. The Packers crunched the Chilar Athletic Club of Chicago and the Maple Leaf Athletic Club of Milwaukee.

14. The American Legion Post of Racine, Wisconsin, sponsored a professional football team that was known as the Racine Legion.

15. After the Packers had finished mopping up the field with 10 straight opponents, Lambeau and Calhoun arranged a match with the undefeated Beloit Fairies for the mythical state title.

16. The Fairies took their nickname from the Morse-Fairbanks company, a large manufacturing firm that still exists.

17. Beloit defeated the Packers, 6-0, in a hard-fought contest which could have a different result, Calhoun claimed in the newspaper, if the referee had been unbiased.

18. Tickets weren't sold that first year. Like the year before and like his predecessors did in the two decades before that, Calhoun passed through the crowd asking for donations, which he and the players divided up equally at the end of the season, each man getting a whopping $16.75 for their efforts that year.

19. The Indian Packing Corporation was sold to the Acme Packing Company, a division of the Rival Dog Food Company of Chicago.

20. The boss at the Acme Packing Company was John Clair.

21. Some of the teams that the Packers crushed the first year refused to play them again the next season. Thus, Lambeau was forced to schedule their two toughest opponents for home-and-away pairings. Those two teams were the Beloit Fairies and the miners from Stambaugh.

22. Playing Marinette, Wisconsin, and Menominee, Michigan, two towns divided only by the Menominee River and a state line, had been a fall tradition for Green Bay since the 1890s.

23. Lambeau scheduled the Lapham Athletic Club of Milwaukee and the Boosters Athletic Club of Chicago.

24. Calhoun "hurled the defy", a period expression meaning "challenged", at the sportswriters of Milwaukee to put the best eleven on the field to face the Packers from little Green Bay, and the Milwaukee scribes responded by fielding an all-star team of the best players in the local athletic club circuit. With more practice together, they might have beaten the Packers, but Lambeau's squad defeated them, 9-0.

25. The Chicago Boosters held Green Bay to a 3-3 tie. Beloit gained a split in their two games with the Pack by winning the second game, 14-7. And the Menominee squad managed to score a single TD in their 19-7 loss to the Packers.

3 - The Packers Join the NFL

1. The name of the first organization was the American Professional Football Association.

2. The APFA was founded Sept. 17, 1920.

3. The APFA was founded in the showroom of Ralph Hay's Hupmobile car dealership in Canton, Ohio.

4. Rochester, New York; Hammond and Muncie, Indiana; Decatur, Chicago, and Rock Island, Illinois; Akron, Cleveland, Canton, Massillon, and Dayton, Ohio.

5. The founders elected Jim Thorpe in absentia because he had the most recognizable name in professional football at the time.

6. The Acme Packing Company sponsored the Packers in 1921.

7. The NFL granted this franchise to John and Emmett Clair of the Acme Packing Co.

8. The Clair brothers received their franchise on August 27, 1921.

9. Prior to playing other pro teams in the new league, the Packers played the Boosters Athletic Club of Chicago, Rockford, the Cornell-Hamburg Athletic Club of Chicago, and the Fairbanks-Morse team of Beloit, defeating all four with shutouts.

10. The Rock Island Independents visited Green Bay in October and went home 10-3 victors.

11. The Minneapolis Marines, Evansville Crimson Giants, and Hammond Pros were Green Bay's victims.

12. The next contest for the Packers was against the oldest professional team in the history of pro football. This team started in 1906 as the Racine Street Athletic Club. George Halas and several others supposedly in the know about the history of the game have confused this team with the Racine (Wis.) Legion. They came to be known as the Chicago Cardinals. The Packers played them to a 3-3 tie in their first ever meeting.

13. Calhoun beat the drums for the Packers when they faced the Staleys in Chicago, but to no avail as the Halasmen dumped Green Bay, 20-0.

14. Calhoun came up with the idea of the Packers playing the Racine Legion for the state title, and a game was arranged for early December at Athletic Park in Milwaukee. The game ended in a 3-3 tie, settling nothing. A rematch the next Sunday was canceled because of a snowstorm, and a second effort to determine the title was also erased by Mother Nature. A plan to play the game indoors after Christmas was scrubbed, leaving the mythical title undecided.

15. The answer here is questionable. Some authorities say Green Bay's opponent was the Racine Legion in the so-called title game in Milwaukee. My opinion and research say it was the Chicago Staleys, whom the Packers played the week before in Chicago.

16. All three played for Notre Dame.

17. Of the three, the most famous was Heartly "Hunk" Anderson, a native of Michigan's Upper Peninsula.

18. No one ever came forth and took credit for exposing Lambeau, but every indication pointed to George Halas as the unnamed source in the newspaper stories. Allegedly, the Staleys were the only team then not using college players. The only person who would say that was Halas.

19. At the league meeting, the Clair brothers were asked to surrender their franchise, and Emmett Clair did just that, leaving Green Bay without a

team in the league.

20. After Clair forfeited the franchise, Lambeau had the effrontery to request that it be granted to him.

21. Lambeau attended every league meeting to put forth his case to have a franchise granted to him.

22. The National Football League granted a franchise to Earl L. Lambeau on August 21, 1922. To gain this piece of paper, he had to post a bond of $1,000 to be paid in cash before receiving the actual franchise document. He came up with the money, and Green Bay had a professional team again.

23. The corporation was legally known as "The Green Bay Football Club".

24. Joining Lambeau as incorporators were Nathan Abrams, Joe Ordens, and George Whitney Calhoun.

25. In an attempt to make a little extra money to pay the bills, the Packers scheduled a non-league game with the Duluth Kellys. The weather didn't co-operate that day as rain fell throughout the night and well into the next morning. Lambeau, Calhoun, Abrams, and Ordens were faced with going ahead with the game and losing a lot of money or canceling the affair and losing a lot of money.

26. Andrew B. Turnbull, business manager for the Green Bay *Press-Gazette*, advised Lambeau and friends to play the game with the Kellys. If they didn't, professional football in Green Bay would be dead forever.

27. They played the game in a steady rain before less than 100 fans, and the Packers won a meaningless game, 10-0.

28. Turnbull told them to play the game, and if they did, he would do something to save pro football for Green Bay.

29. The brilliant lawyer who saved pro football for Green Bay on this occasions was named Gerald F. Clifford.

30. The Green Bay Football Corporation.

31. Turnbull and Clifford enlisted businessman Leland Joannes, Dr. W. Weber Kelly, and John Kittell, the president of the local Elks Club.

32. The price was $5.00 a share.

33. The incorporation papers called for a board of 15 directors.

34. The board of directors elected Andrew B. Turnbull as the first president of the Green Bay Football Corporation.

35. Joining Turnbull on the executive committee were John Kittell as the first vice-president, Leland Joannes as the first secretary-treasurer, and Dr. W. Weber Kelly and

George DeLair as members at-large.

36. Lambeau was placed in charge of football operations, and Calhoun was elected to be team secretary. Ordens and Abrams were left out in the cold.

4 - A Few Good Men

1. April 9, 1898.

2. Marcel.

3. Marcel Lambeau was a construction contractor.

4. The Lambeau family emigrated to northeastern Wisconsin from Belgium in the 1870s.

5. Curly attended East High School where he starred in football and track.

6. Curly graduated from high school in 1917, and that fall he went off to college in Madison to the University of Wisconsin. He got homesick and came home after a month.

7. Being Catholic and loving football, Curly took a shot at playing for Notre Dame in 1918.

8. Curly's famous running mate in the Notre Dame backfield was none other than the immortal George Gipp.

9. Notre Dame and George Gipp can only add up to Knute Rockne being Curly's coach.

10. He went home for Christmas with a case of tonsillitis, stayed to have them out, and never went back to college because he got a great job at the Indian Packing Corporation plant in Green Bay.

11. Curly married Marguerite Van Kessel August 16, 1919.

12. Curly was the foreman of the loading dock, where he earned $250 a month. (Or so one source reported. More than likely he was making $2.50 a day or about 25 cents an hour which was still good pay for a 20-years-old man in 1919.)

13. Curly was an original inductee into the Pro Football Hall of Fame in 1963.

14. Curly was original inductee into the Packer Hall of Fame in 1970.

15. September 16, 1890.

16. Cal was descended from Daniel Whitney, Green Bay's first non-French settler, who established Washington House, Green Bay's first known tavern.

17. Buffalo (N,Y,) University

18. He played football, hockey, and lacrosse.

19. In his senior year at college, Cal developed juvenile arthritis that left his hands gnarled and his legs gimpy for the rest of his life.

20. The Green Bay *Press-Gazette*.

21. Cal was the business manager for the town team in 1918, and he held the same position for the Packers in the years before Green Bay joined the APFA.

22. Cal was inducted into the Packer Hall of Fame in 1978 for his role as publicity director in the early days of the organization.

23. Turnbull was born in London, Ontario, Canada.

24. Turnbull moved to the Detroit, Michigan, with his family when he was a youngster. He came to Green Bay in 1915.

25. Turnbull worked for newspapers wherever he went. In Green Bay, he worked for the *Press-Gazette*.

26. Turnbull served at business manager for the *Press-Gazette*.

27. Turnbull was the first president of the non-profit corporation that began operating the Packers in 1923.

28. Turnbull Was inducted into the Packer Hall of Fame for his service as president of the corporation, 1923-27.

29. Gerald Clifford was born in Escanaba, Michigan, just 100 miles up the west shore of Lake Michigan from Green Bay.

30. W. Weber Kelly was born in Jamaica, educated in England and Canada, and practiced medicine in the United States.

31. Leland Joannes was a partner in Joannes Brothers Wholesale Groceries.

32. Clifford served on the board of directors and the executive committee from the time of its inception until his death.

33. Kelly resigned over a dispute with Lambeau in the '40s.

34. Joannes served as president of the corporation from 1930 thru 1947.

35. Joannes was inducted into the packer Hall of Fame in 1981 for service as president of the Packer corporation for 18 years.

36. Kelly served as president of the corporation for one year, 1929.

37. Clifford was inducted into the Packer Hall of Fame in 1991.

38. Clifford was the lawyer who wrote the articles of incorporation that made it virtually impossible for the Packers to be sold or moved to another city.

5 - The First Triple Champs

1. In 1921, Lambeau learned the former Wisconsin tackle Howard "Cub" Buck had taken a job in nearby Appleton. Buck had played for the Canton Bulldogs the year before, and after the Bulldogs concluded their season, he played for the Lapham Athletic Club of Milwaukee. He was

so dominating that Lambeau picked Buck as the man to build a real pro team around.

2. In 1922, Lambeau raided other teams for players. He started by talking Howard "Whitey" Woodin, a guard who had played his college ball at Marquette, to jump the Racine Legion and come to Green Bay.

3. Louis Francis Earpe played football for little Monmouth College in Illinois. Afterward, he played for the Rock Island Independents, but a dispute with that team's management allowed him to join the Packers in the middle of the season.

4. Lyle "Cowboy" Wheeler, an end at Ripon College, was the last holdover from the old city team. He played his final game for the Packers in 1923.

5. Charley Mathys grew up in Green Bay and went to West High School. He played one year with the Hammond Pros in 1921 before joining the Packers in 1922.

6. The 1921 Packers played only a few quality teams in the APFA (NFL), losing to two of them and tying the other to gain a final mark of 3-2-1. The competition improved in 1922, and so did the Packers who finished at 4-3-3. After starting slow in 1923, the Packers won their last five games to finish third in the NFL standings at 7-2-1.

7. Vern Lewellen graduated from Nebraska and came to Green Bay to

practice law and play football for the Packers. He could pass, punt, and run the ball with the best of them.

8. Dick O'Donnell played for Minnesota in college, then joined the Duluth Kellys for one year before signing with the Packers in 1924.

9. Eddie Kotal played his college ball at little Lawrence College in Appleton, Wisconsin.

10. Carl "Cully" "Swede" Lidberg came out of Minnesota with the reputation for being a crunching runner.

11. The 1924 team finished sixth in a league of 18 teams with a record of 7-4. The next season the Packers dropped to ninth in a field of 20 with a mark of 8-5. 1926 saw them finish fifth out of 22 teams with a 7-3-3 record.

12. Lambeau signed Bernard "Boob" Darling, a center from little Beloit (Wis.) College; Richard "Red" Smith, a guard from nearby Kaukauna, Wisconsin, who had played at Notre Dame; and Claude Perry, a tackle from Dixie who went to college at Alabama.

13. When the Milwaukee Badgers went to ground after the 1926 season, LaVern Dilweg, an end out of Marquette, became available, and Lambeau signed him.

14. After playing out his college days for Marquette, Dunn played for the Milwaukee Badgers, then the

Chicago Cardinals.

15. Roger Ashmore played for the Duluth Eskimos in their last season in the NFL, and Paul Minick came aboard after the Buffalo Bisons became extinct.

16. Tom Nash played for the Packers for five years, including all three of the Triple Champs.

17. The Packers came close to a title in 1927, finishing second to the Giants with a mark of 7-2-1 in a league of 12. Then they slipped to fourth in 1928 with a record of 6-4-3 when the NFL had been reduced to 10 teams.

18. Cal Hubbard played for the New York Giants in 1927-28.

19. Hubbard attended classes at little Centenary and Geneva Colleges.

20. Hubbard became a Major League Baseball umpire after his NFL career came to an end.

21. Hubbard is the only man in the history of professional sports to be inducted into the Pro Football Hall of Fame, the Baseball Hall of Fame, and the Packer Hall of Fame. Besides being one of the most feared tackles of his time, he became one of the most respected umpires in Baseball.

22. Michalske's college was Penn State.

23. Michalske signed with C.C. Pyle's New York Yankees of the first American Football League in 1926. He continued to play for New York after the AFL folded and the Yankees joined the NFL in 1927, but when Pyle abandoned the team after the 1928 season, Michalske became a free agent and signed with the Packers.

24. Michalske was given the name of August at birth. With a first name like that, it's easy to see how he became "Iron Mike" Michalske in the NFL.

25. Johnny Blood's real name was John McNally.

26. John McNally was born in New Richmond, Wisconsin, the "wayward" son in a wealthy family. He took the name of Johnny Blood from a theatre marquee where the film *Blood and Sand* was playing. He took the alias in order to play pro football on Sundays because he was still attending college during the rest of the week.

27. Blood attended college at St. John's (Minn.). He enrolled at Notre Dame but left to play pro ball.

28. Blood played for the Milwaukee Badgers, the Duluth Eskimos, and the Pottsville Maroons before hopping a freight for Green Bay in 1929.

29. After a dispute with Lambeau, Blood went to the Pittsburgh Pirates (Steelers later), returned to the Packers for two years, then went back to Pittsburgh to finish out his career.

30. McCrary went to Georgia.

31. Molenda signed with the New York Yankees in 1927 and also played for them in 1928.

32. Molenda went to Michigan.

33. Molenda joined the New York Giants in 1933 and finished his career there in 1935.

34. The Packers completed a near perfect season with a mark of 12-0-1, the tie coming at the hands of the Frankford Yellow Jackets.

35. The native son was Green Bay's own Arnie Herber, a curly headed look alike of Lambeau who became Lambeau's protégé.

36. Herber attended college at little Regis College in Colorado before dropping out in the fall of 1930 to join the Packers.

37. A veteran of 14 years in the NFL Herber was inducted into the Hall of Fame in 1966.

38. Sleight went to Purdue.

39. Engelmann went to South Dakota State.

40. The Packers won the NFL title in 1930 with a mark of 10-3-1, winning all their home games for the second straight year.

41. Bruder played all but one year of his pro career with the Packers, and Gantenbein played his entire pro career in Green Bay.

42. Bruder went to Northwester, while Gantenbein attended Wisconsin. Grove went to Michigan State, but the Spartans were not a member of the Big 10 in those years.

43. Gantenbein played end, and Comstock played guard.

44. Comstock was a Hoya from Georgetown.

45. The Packers finished their third straight championship season with a 12-2 record. For the three years, the Packers were an incredible 34-5-2.

46. The Packers' '32 mark was 10-3-1.

47. Lambeau took the team on a post-season barnstorming tour to Hawaii and California.

48. Blood arranged the trip to Hawaii.

49. Blood was a newspaper reporter on the trip for the Green Bay *Press-Gazette*.

50. Lambeau arranged for Red Grange to play for the Packers in the California portion Of the tour.

6 - The Hutson Era
1. The Bears defeated Portsmouth, 9-0.

2. The game was played inside Chicago Stadium.

3. The goal posts were moved to

the goal line to emphasize the kicking game. Hash marks were put on the field. The passing rule was changed to allow passers to throw from anywhere behind the line of scrimmage instead of having to be five yards deep to pass. All three of these rules opened up the game to higher scoring and more excitement. Punting declined, and attendance increased throughout the league.

4. The Packers finished the year with a dismal 5-7-1 mark.

5. The corporation was forced into bankruptcy by a fan who sued it for injuries he suffered when he fell from the bleachers in a game in 1931.

6. Corporation lawyer Gerald Clifford convinced the court to appoint a friendly receiver in the person of Frank Jonet, a certified public accountant who was also a stockholder in the corporation.

7. The corporation held another stock sale, raised enough money to pay off the bankruptcy, and started a new corporation known as Green Bay Packers, Inc.

8. Buckets Goldenberg, 1972; Bobby Monnett, 1973; and Lon Evans, 1978.

9. Smith, end; Kurth and Quatse, tackles; Greeney and Evans, guards; Sarafiny and Young, centers.

10. Goldenberg, Monnett, and Evans. All the others from 1933 left the Packers after that year.

11. Laws, 1972; Johnston, 1981; and Engebretsen, 1978.

12. Laws, Johnston, and Casper.

13. Engebretsen, Schwammel, Laws, Seibold, Johnston, and Butler.

14. Svendsen and Hutson.

15. Maddox, tackle; Smith; tackle; Tenner, end; Vairo, end; O'Connor, tackle; Svendsen, center; and—oh, yes—Hutson, end.

16. Smith, Sauer, Schneidman, Svendsen, and—oh, yes—Hutson.

17. Letlow is the only member of the class of '36 to be inducted into the Packer Hall of Fame.

18. Miller, Clemens, and Mattos.

19. The Packers finished in third place in 1934 and second place the next year.

20. The Packers went from 7-6-0 in 1934 to 8-4-0 in 1935, then won it all in 1936 with a record of 10-1-1.

21. Eddie Jankowski, 1984; and Earl "Bud" Svendsen, 1985.

22. Jankowski, Peterson ,and Banet.

23. Jankowski and Svendsen.

24. All five were inducted into the Packer Hall of Fame: Isbell, 1972; Ray, 1973; Uram, 1973; Tinsley, 1979; and Mulleneaux, 1983.

25. Tinsley, guard; Ray, tackle; and Mulleneaux, end.

26. All five played on the title team.

27. Charley Brock and Larry Craig were inducted into the Hall of Fame in 1973, and Harry Jacunski was voted into the Hall in 1991.

28. Craig, Buhler, and Balazs.

29. In 1937, the Packers finished in a tie for second with a record of 7-4-0. In 1938, the Packers won one more game than the previous year to win the division with a mark of 8-3-0. In 1939, the Packers lost two game, both by a field goal, and they won the division with a record of 9-2-0.

30. Tony Canadeo, 1973; Ted Fritsch, 1973; Lou Brock, 1982; and Irv Comp, 1986.

31. Fritsch attended college at Central State Teachers College, now UW-Stevens Point.

32. Comp attended classes at St. Benedict.

33. Mason, end; Berezney, tackle; and Croft, tackle.

34. Comp, Perkins, and McKay.

35. Kercher, end; Tollefson, guard; and Wehba, end.

36. The Packers finished second in the division in 1940 with a 6-4-1 record; tied for first in '41 at 10-10-0; second in '42 at 8-2-1; second in '43

at 7-2-1; and first in '44 with a mark of 8-2-0.

37. Bucknell. You had to be there.

38. Hinkle wasn't merely a running back; he was a power runner, a true fullback.

39. Hinkle was the linebacker in Lambeau's 6-1-4 defensive scheme.

40. Hinkle held the career rushing records for most yards (3,860), most attempts (1,171), and most field goals made (28).

41. Hinkle was among the second group to be inducted into the Pro Football Hall of Fame in 1964.

42. Hinkle was among the second group of great Packers to be inducted into the Packer Hall of Fame in 1972.

43. Hinkle played for the Packers for 10 years from 1932 thru 1941.

44. Hinkle was selected to the All-Pro team four times: '36, '37, '38, and '41.

45. Hutson went to Alabama, going there because a friend wanted him along.

46. This was too easy. End.

47. Not so easy. Halfback. Today he would be called a cornerback.

48. Hutson held every pass receiving record as well as most touchdowns scored, most extra

points kicked, and most points scored.

49. Hutson was a member of the first group of players selected to the Pro Football Hall of Fame in 1964.

50. Believe it or not, Hutson was not selected in the first group of Packers to be inducted into the Packer Hall of Fame. He was a member of the second group in 1972.

51. Hutson played for the Packers for 11 years from 1935 thru 1945.

52. Hutson was All-Pro nine of his 11 season in the NFL: 1936 and 1938-1945.

7 - The Fall of Curly Lambeau
1. The two paper leagues were the United States Football League and the Trans-America Football League.

2. Red Grange was hired to organize and lead the USFL.

3. This unsuccessful league was the fourth American Football League.

4. The winner in the new league pool was the All-America Football Conference.

5. Former member of the "Four Horsemen of Notre Dame" Jimmy Crowley was elected to be the AAC's first president.

6. The AAC began play in 1946.

7. The AAC started with eight teams: New York Yankees, Brooklyn Dodgers, Miami Seahawks, Buffalo Bisons, Cleveland Browns, Chicago Rockets, Los Angeles Dons, and San Francisco 49ers.

8. The backers of the Miami Seahawks couldn't sustain their financial losses and were forced to surrender their franchise.

9. A new franchise was granted to entrepreneurs in Baltimore, and they nicknamed their team the Colts.

10. The Buffalo Bisons changed their name to the Buffalo Bills.

11. The New York Yankees and Brooklyn Dodgers became the New York-Brooklyn Yankees.

12. The Chicago Rockets became the Hornets for 1949.

13. Cecil Isbell coached the Baltimore Colts.

14. The Cleveland Browns, San Francisco 49ers, and Baltimore Colts became members of the NFL in 1950.

15. Lambeau sent out contracts to over 100 players inn early 1946. The only one who chose to play in the new league was Bob Frankowski, a guard from Washington.

16. Lee Joannes and Lambeau signed a working agreement with the San Diego Bombers of the Pacific Coast League.

17. Lambeau convinced the

executive committee to buy Rockwood Lodge as a training camp for the Packers.

18. Lambeau drafted john Strzykalski, a back out of Marquette who signed with the Cleveland Browns.

19. At the winter meetings in '46, Mara and Marshall tried to convince Joannes and Lambeau to move the Packers to San Francisco to compete with the new league team there.

20. Clarke Hinkle spoke to a high school banquet where he said, "The Green Bay Packers are not going to be in Green Bay very long unless the city's civic organizations wake up and create more interest in the team." This quote was picked up by the wire services, and the rumors that the Packers would be moving to San Francisco or Baltimore or Dallas started flying across the country.

21. Lambeau drafted Ernie Case, a back out of UCLA who signed with the Baltimore Colts of the AAC.

22. Lambeau traded halfback Bob Nussbaumer to the Washington Redskins for Jack Jacobs.

23. Lambeau fired his long-time friend and supporter George Whitney Calhoun as publicity director of the Packers and hired huckster George Strickler.

24. Lee Joannes retired as president of the Packers after 17 years at the helm. He cited the demands of a new business as the reason for stepping down, but the truth was he and Lambeau were at odds with each other over several matters.

25. The Packers had beaten the Steelers nine straight games since Art Rooney was granted a franchise for Pittsburgh in 1933, but since then, the Steelers have won 11 of 20 games with Green Bay.

26. Lambeau began negotiating a contract to coach the Los Angeles Dons in '48.

27. Emil Fischer, new president of the Packers, held Lambeau to his contract to coach the Packers.

28. Lambeau drafted and signed Earl "Jug" Girard, a back from Wisconsin, but he didn't come easy. Girard signed a contract with the New York Yankees of the AAC before reneging on it and signing with Green Bay.

29. Jay Rhodemyre, a center from Kentucky, earned top honors at the College All-Star game in '48.

30. The Packers lost their last seven games, then added tow more losses to the skein in '49 before finally defeating another opponent. This would remain the packers longest losing streak in their history.

31. The Packers finished in last place in '49 with a mark of 2-10. This was the worst record in Green Bay's history and the first time the team

ended up in the division cellar.

32. Rockwood Lodge burned to the ground on January 25, 1950, and the insurance money helped save the franchise from extinction.

33. The board of directors voted 21-3 for renewing Lambeau's coaching contract for 1950. Those voting against him were Jerry Clifford, George W. Calhoun, and Dr. W. W. Kelly, whom Lambeau had fired as team physician a few years earlier.

34. The man cited as a co-conspirator in Lambeau's attempt to regain control of the Packers was Vic McCormick, a wealthy member of the board of directors.

35. History has finally decided that Gerald Clifford, the Packers' attorney, prevented Lambeau from regaining the franchise by investigating Lambeau's activities and learning that Lambeau had abused his expense account.

36. Lambeau resigned from his posts with the corporation on January 31, 1950. At the same time, he announced that he had signed a new deal with the Chicago Cardinals to be that team's coach and general manager for the coming year. He lasted less than two years before taking a hike with two games left to play in the '51 season.

PACKER THIS 'N' DATA

1 - FIRSTS

1. Technically, Bill Ryan was the coach, but this is deceptive. In the early days of football, the coach on the sidelines did not run the team; the captain on the field ran the team. On the 1919 team, Curly Lambeau was the captain, the man in charge. If "coach" is defined as the man in charge, then Curly Lambeau was the coach.

2. See answer #1 above. The same applies to the 1921 team. Lambeau was the captain, the man in charge on the field. The coach on the sidelines was Joe Hoeffel.

3. This is a deceiving question because the position of quarterback in the early days of the packers was not the same as it is today. The quarterback called the signals, but he seldom handled the ball. He threw the ball even less because his primary job was blocking for the other backs. Jim Coffeen did a lot of that on the 1919 Packers as well as for earlier town teams.

4. See answer #2 above and substitute Norm Barry for Jim Coffeen and 1921 for 1919.

5. The Packers had several scouts before Jack Vainisi was hired in 1950, but none of them came close to achieving the success he had at finding talent for the Packers.

6. Russ Winnie did play-by-play recreations of the games from ticker tape new on radio station WTMJ in Milwaukee in 1929.

7. In 1930, radio station WHBY in Green Bay carried Packer broadcasts with Harold T.I. Shannon and Hal Lansing providing the play-by-play reporting.

8. The Packers played four non-league teams before meeting the Rock Island (Ill.) Independents October 23, 1921, in Green Bay, losing 13-3.

9. The Packers first NFL victim was the Minneapolis Marines, 7-6, October 30, 1921.

10. Hagemeister Park, Green Bay, Wisconsin, September 14, 1919.

11. Hagemeister Park, Green Bay, Wisconsin, October 30, 1921.

12. After starting the NFL campaign with three wins and a loss at home, the Packers traveled to Chicago to play the Cardinals, coming away with a 3-3 tie.

13. The Packers played the Chicago Staleys in 1921, but this team was not the Bears. The Bears didn't come into being until January 28, 1922, when George Halas and his partner were granted their own franchise in the NFL. So the Packers first game against the Bears took place October 14, 1923, in Green Bay.

14. The Giants came into the NFL in

1925, but the Packers didn't play them until October 7, 1928. They did play the New York Yankees in 1927, but they were a different team.

15. The Packers lost their first two encounters with the Bears in 1923 and 1924 by the identical scores of 3-0. They dumped the Bears in Green Bay, September 27, 1925, by the score of 14-10.

16. 1929 (I said it was easy.)

17. After 12 consecutive winning seasons in the NFL, the Packers finally finished a season below .500 in 1933 with a mark of 5-7-1. They would not have another losing until 1948.

18. The NFL divided itself into two divisions, Eastern and Western, in 1933. It took the Packers four years to win their first Western Division crown in 1936.

19. The Packers capped a near-perfect 1936 campaign by thumping the Boston Redskins in the NFL title game, 21-6.

20. The NFL instituted the drafting of college players after the 1935 season. The Packers chose guard Russ Letlow from San Francisco, and he played eight years for Green Bay.

21. The Packers and Bears finished the 1941 season with identical records, 10-1. The Packers only loss was to the Bears, 25-17, in Green Bay; and ironically, the Bears only loss was to the Packers, 16-14, in Chicago. The two teams met in

Chicago to decide the Western Division championship on December 14, 1941, and the Bears went on to play the New York Giants in the NFL title game a week later.

22. The Packers finished in last place for the first time in 1949 with a mark of 2-10, the second worst record in the team's history.

23. 1921.

24. Andrew B. Turnbull.

25. The Packers played the Minnesota Vikings to a 10-10 tie November 26, 1978, at Green Bay. The score was the same after the overtime period.

26. The Packers beat the Vikings for the very first time in their very first meeting October 22, 1961. They beat them a second time October 29, 1961.

27. The Packers beat the Tampa Bay Buccaneers for the very time in their very first meeting October 23, 1977.

28. If you said November 2, 1930, you are wrong because the Lions were the Spartans of Portsmouth, Ohio, then. The question asked when the Packers beat the *Detroit Lions* for the first time. The Packers defeated the Detroit Lions for the very first time in their second meeting November 25, 1934.

29. September 24, 1995.

30. Although the Packers have played the Cleveland Browns, they have yet to play the Baltimore Ravens. It's complicated. The Ravens owner, Art Modell, wants to shed the past, and the Cleveland people want another team, an expansion team, that will be named the Browns and will continue with the history of the old Cleveland Browns. I said it was complicated.

2 - POST SEASON PLAY

1. The Packers tied the Bears for first place in the Western Division in 1941, forcing a playoff game.

2. The Bears defeated the Packers, 33-14, at Chicago.

3. The Packers corralled the Baltimore Colts, 13-10, at Green Bay.

4. The Packers dumped the Dallas Cowboys, 34-27, at the Cotton Bowl in Dallas.

5. Only two weeks earlier in Los Angeles, the Packers lost to the Rams, 27-24; but when they met in Milwaukee, December 23, the Packers destroyed the Rams, 28-7.

6. December 31, 1967.

7. The Dallas Cowboys won the right to freeze their butts in Green Bay by winning the Capitol Division and slamming the Cleveland Browns in the first round, 52-14.

8. The temperature registered a balmy 13 degrees below zero with winds gusting up to 15 miles per hour or so said one report.

9. The "Ice Bowl" was Vince Lombardi's last game in Green Bay as head coach.

10. The Cowboys only coach from 1960 until Jimmy Johnson replaced him in 1989 was the legendary Tom Landry.

11. None other than quarterback turned football announcer turned actor "Dandy" Don Meredith.

12. Boyd Dowler scored both TDS.

13. Too easy. Bart Starr.

14. The final score: Green Bay 21, Dallas 17.

15. 50,861 of the hardiest, bravest souls in the whole country, with the exceptions of some ladies who weren't quite the fans that their husbands were.

16. I have personally spoken to 252,149 people who claim to have survived the "Ice Bowl". (In the last edition of this work, the number was 251,003. Another 1,146 true Packer fans have come forward since then.)

17. Most Packer fans and historians don't want to remember Dan Devine for anything except "The Trade". He directed the Packers to a 10-4 record and first place in the Central Division for their only appearance in post-season play during the whole decade.

18. Another easy one. Bart Starr.

19. The NFL Players Union went on strike after the second game of the season and stayed out eight weeks. The season was shortened to nine games.

20. Instead of having division winners and wild cards in the Playoffs, the NFL chose to have a "Suer Bowl Tournament" that featured the eight best teams in each conference vying for a spot in the Super Bowl. The Packers were seeded fourth in the NFC.

21. The Packers dumped the St. Louis Cardinals, 41-16, in their first Playoff game in Green Bay since the "Ice Bowl" in 1967.

22. The Packers twice eliminated the Cowboys from the Playoffs back in the '60s. Dallas had some revenge when they beat the Packers, 37-26, January 16, 1983.

23. The Packers beat the Detroit Lions at the Pontiac Silver Dome one week after the Lions had beaten the Packers on the same field during the regular season.

24. The Dallas Cowboys really know how to hold a grudge.

25. For the second straight year, the Packers faced the Detroit Lions in the first round of the Playoffs, and again they came away winners, 16-12.

26. The Atlanta Falcons came to Green Bay and went home losers, 37-20.

27. Never. It was the first-ever meeting between the two teams in post-season play.

28. Once. The Packers beat the 49ers in the Divisional Playoff in 1996.

29. Dickey threw four TD passes in the rout to tie the Playoff record.

30. Carolina Panthers.

31. James Lofton ran an end-around for 71 yards, tying the Playoff record for longest run from scrimmage.

32. New York Giants.

33. The Packers and the Giants have met five times for the NFL title.

34. The New York Giants beat the Packers, 23-17, in New York, December 11, 1938; and the Philadelphia Eagles slipped by the Packers, 17-13, December 26, 1960.

35. Curly Lambeau.

36. Vince Lombardi won five, and Mike Holmgren has won one so far.

37. 1929, 1930, 1931, 1936, 1939, 1944, 1961, 1962, 1965, 1966, 1967, and 1996.

38. The 1936 game was played at the Polo Grounds in New York.

39. Boston Redskins.

40. 28 years (1968 thru 1995).

41. If you got question #30 right, then you should know that the Packers played the New York Giants in those five games. A little lesson in deductive reasoning.

42. State Fair Park. West Allis, Wis. Milwaukee is also an acceptable answer.

43. Each Packer collected a whopping $540 for winning, which was about nine weeks pay for most working men in those days.

44. The Packers and the New York Giants drew only 39,029 fans to their 1961 title game, but the ticket prices were so high that they brought in over a million dollars.

45. Los Angeles Memorial Coliseum.

46. Green Bay 35, Kansas City 10.

47. The Oakland Raiders won the AFL crown and the right to be humbled by the Packers in Super Bowl II.

48. Green Bay 33, Oakland 14.

49. Each player was paid $15,000 for playing in Super Bowl I.

50. New England Patriots.

51. The Superdome, New Orleans, Louisiana.

52. Green Bay Packers 35, New England Patriots 21.

53. Desmond Howard.

54. Bart Starr.

55. Bart Starr.

56. Desmond Howard broke the record for most punt return yards, and this was alos the team record. For the record, the official record is called *Most Yards, Punt Returns, Game: 90, Green Bay.*

57. Twice: once after the 1963 season and once after the 1964 season.

58. The Packers beat the Cleveland Browns in 1963.

59. The Packers lost to the St. Louis Cardinals in 1964.

60. I have personally talked to 252,149 fans who claim to care.

3- GREEN BAY VS. CHICAGO

1. Chicago athletic clubs began playing football against each other before the 19th Century ended. Some of these clubs ventured outside Chicago occasionally. The one that came to Green Bay in 1919 was the Chilar Athletic Club.

2. Chicago had its own semi-pro league for a long time, and one of its premier teams was the Boosters.

3. The Cornell-Hamburg Athletic Club of Chicago has been mistakenly

identified as the Chicago Cornhuskers by some historians.

4. The Staleys took their name from their sponsor, the A.E. Staley Starch Company of Decatur, Ill. Actually, the Staleys of 1920 played only a few games in Decatur, while playing a majority of their home schedule in Chicago.

5. George Halas played end, coached the line, and was also head coach of the Staleys.

6. The founder of the team that became known as the Cardinals was painting and decorating contractor Chris O'Brien.

7. O'Brien organized his club as the Morgan Athletic Club in 1898 or 1899, depending on which source you read.

8. Legend has it that O'Brien bought some secondhand jerseys from the University of Chicago. The jerseys were originally maroon in color but had faded to a dark red, a cardinal color. If they had faded any more, the team might have been called the Reds instead of the Cardinals. This is doubtful because even back then Reds was an unsavory name attached to communists, socialists, anarchists, and others militant political activists. Just a little history lesson.

9. O'Brien's team played its home games on a field located at the corner of Normal Boulevard and Racine Street on Chicago's South Side; thus,

they were known as the Normals.

10. After playing four other NFL foes, the Packers played the Cardinals in Chicago November 20, 1921, holding the Cardinals to a 3-3 tie.

11. After four losses and a tie, the Packers finally beat the Cardinals in Chicago, 3-0, October 31, 1926.

12. The Packers were the first NFL team to play the Cardinals at Comiskey Park, October 15, 1926.

13. From 1934 thru 1936, the Packers and Cardinals played each other three times a year in regular season action; once each in Green Bay, Chicago, and Milwaukee, with each team calling the Milwaukee contest a home game in alternating years.

14. After playing the first game in 1938 in Milwaukee on Sunday September 25, 1938, both teams boarded a train for Buffalo, New York, where they played a mid-week game, Wednesday, September 28, 1938.

15. The Cardinals and Steelers merged for the 1944 season and were known as Card-Pitt instead of Chi-Pitt in order to make it clear that it was the Cardinals and not the Bears who were merged with the Steelers.

16. The Cardinals won the NFL title in 1947.

17. The first quarterback in the Packers' NFL history was Norm

Barry. He was the coach who led the Cardinals to their first NFL title in 1925.

18. After being forced to leave the Packers in early 1950, Curly Lambeau signed on with the Cardinals for the 1950 and 1951 seasons, but he quit the team after 10 games of the 1951 season because of a running battle with the club's management.

19. One of the greatest all-around backs in NFL history, Paddy Driscoll, was the player-coach of the Cardinals for their first three seasons in the NFL.

20. Dr. David Jones, a Chicago dentist, bought the Cardinals from Chris O'Brien in 1929. After four years of losing money, he sold the club to tycoon Charles W. Bidwill who poured his heart and money into the Cardinals. Bidwill died of a heart attack April 19, 1947.

21. Before the 1922 season, Lambeau made a contract with the Bears to play them in Green Bay on Thanksgiving Day. The Monday before Turkey Day Halas wired Lambeau and demanded a guarantee of $4,000 to come to Green Bay. The Packers hadn't taken in $4,000 in gate receipts for any game that year, so they had to say no dice to Halas. He then refused to come to Green Bay, and the game had to be canceled. In an effort to make some money for that day, Lambeau made a quick deal with the Duluth Kellys to come to Green Bay to play a non-league game on Thanksgiving Day,

and you know what happened then.

Just imagine what might have happened if Halas hadn't tried to gouge the Packers for more money. The Bears would have come to Green Bay on that rainy day in 1922, and because it was a league game, Lambeau wouldn't have even considered canceling it; Calhoun, Ordens, Abrams, and he wouldn't have met at the offices of the *Press-Gazette*; and Andrew Turnbull wouldn't have been made aware of their financial plight. The end result would have been the disappearance of the Green Bay Packers from the face of the earth.

But that's not what happened because George Halas was greedy.

22. The first time the Packers played the Bears in Chicago was November 23, 1924.

23. It took the Packers six trips to Chicago before they defeated the Bears, 16-6, October 21, 1928.

24. Same year, 1928. After playing to a 12-12 tie in Green Bay early in the year, the Packers beat the Bears in Chicago in October and on December 9.

25. The Packers and Bears were scheduled to play each other three times a year in 1926, then from 1928 thru 1933. The Packers beat the Bears in all three games in 1929.

26. The Bears beat the Packers twice in 1926.

27. The Bears won all three

meetings with the Packers in 1933.

28. The Packers and Bears met in Milwaukee November 10, 1974, and the Packers won, 20-3.

29. The Packers beat the Bears seven straight times from 1928 thru 1930.

30. The Packers won the second game in 1984, then didn't beat the Bears again until the first game of 1989. In between, the Packers lost eight straight to Mike Ditka's Bears.

31. The Packers played the Bears every year for 59 straight years before the 1982 strike ended the streak.

32. The Packers and Bears met in the pre-season Shrine Game for 15 straight years.

33. Just one time, September 2, 1980.

34. Chester Marcol attempted a field goal in the only overtime game between the Packers and Bears. The Bears blocked it—right back into the startled Marcol's arms and he ran for a TD to win the game.

35. Ray "Scooter" McLean lost both games to the Bears in the one year he coached the Packers.

36. Eight times, including the six in a row thru 1996.

37. The Packers are 2-1 against the Bears on Halloween. Oddly, the score of the game the Packers lost to the Bears was 31-10, the same as the day and month of the year. Pretty spooky, don't you think?

4 - OTHER OPPONENTS

1. The Packers lost two of three contests to the Fairbanks-Morse Fairies of Beloit, Wis., in 1919 and 1920.

2. The Packers put the hurt on the Rockford Maroons, 49-0.

3. The Packers played the Racine Legion in Milwaukee in the game where Lambeau allegedly used college players.

4. The Duluth Kellys hosted the Packers in September, and the Packers returned to favor in November.

5. The Packers prepared for the 1923 season by defeating the Hibbing (Minn.) Miners.

6. Iron Mountain UPers came to Green Bay in 1924, 1925, and 1926 to play the Packers.

7. The Minneapolis Marines joined the NFL at the same time that the Packers did, but the Minnesota fans wouldn't support a loser. The Marines surrendered to failure after four years in the NFL.

8. The Portsmouth Spartans joined the NFL in 1930.

9. The Fort Atkinson Blackhawks

used players from Whitewater Teachers College against the Packers in 1934.

10. In an attempt to raise some badly needed cash and build fan support in the center and western portions of the state, the Packers played the Merrill Fromm Foxes, Chippewa Falls Marines, Stevens Point, and LaCrosse Old Style Lagers—all within nine days—and beat them all soundly.

11. The Packers pounded the Crimson Giants of Evansville, Indiana, 43-6, in 1921.

12. The Panhandles called Columbus, Ohio, their home.

13. The packers beat the Blues, 16-0, in Green Bay, and 17-6, in Kansas City.

14. An original member of the NFL the Rochester Jefferson visited Green Bay in 1925 and went home 33-13 losers.

15. The Providence Steam Roller entered the NFL in 1925, climbed to the top in 1928, then folded after the 1931 season, a year in which the Packers crushed them twice, 48-20 and 38-7.

16. The Frankford Yellow Jackets took their name from a section of Philadelphia. The Great Depression brought about a reversal in their fortunes on the field and at the gate, resulting in the franchise being sold to Bert Bell who restructured the

team and renamed it the Philadelphia Eagles.

17. The Steelers entered the NFL as the Pittsburgh Pirates.

18. The Packers contributed two defeats to the demise of the Detroit Panthers in 1926.

19. Tigers and Dodgers.

20. The Packers were a perfect 10-0 against the Tigers and Dodgers.

21. Cleveland.

22. None of them ever beat or teid the Packers.

23. The Cardinals have yet to beat the Packers since moving to Arizona.

24. The Packers are 4-1 against the San Diego Chargers. If you said Seattle Seahawks, you are incorrect because the Seahawks didn't come into existence for several years after the merger of the AFL and NFL in 1970. The Packers are .500 or worse against every other old AFC team.

25. Five: Giants, Yankees, Yanks, Bulldogs, and Jets.

26. None. The Packers have never been embarrassed by an expansion team. The Bears can't say that.

27. Once. The Packers lost their opener to the Rams in 1995. It was the Rams' first win as the St. Louis Rams.

28. One too many, meaning two in all: the Texans and the Cowboys.

29. 21: Wisconsin, Illinois, Minnesota, Missouri, Texas, Arizona, California, Washington, Indiana, Ohio, Michigan, Pennsylvania, New Jersey, New York, Massachuestts, Colorado, Rhode Island, Maryland, Georgia, Florida, and Louisiana. If you counted the Redskins, remember that Washington is in the District of Columbia, which is not a state. Also, the New York Giants and the New York Jets play their games at the Meadowlands in New Jersey. And Rhode Island? Let us not forget the Providence Steamroller.

30. New York has had five teams that have played the Packers over the decades.

31. The Packers are zip and eight with the Miami Dolphins.

32. The Packers have only won one of three games against the Indianapolis Colts.

33. The Packers have won four of six encounters with the Browns since they were moved into the AFC.

34. The Packers have beaten the Steelers three times in seven meetings since the merger of the AFL and NFL.

35. George Whitney Calhoun was the sports editor for the Green Bay *Press-Gazette* when the Packers started playing teams from Chicago in those early years. He lit the match of

hatred against the big city teams, then he fanned the flames in the coming years.

36. Hal Griffen.

37. Potsy Clark. No, he wasn't Potsy Webber's uncle.

38. 1935. They went on to win the NFL title, too.

39. The 1950s when Bobby Layne was the best quarterback in the NFL, drunk or sober.

40. 1967 when the NFL expanded to 16 teams.

41. Norm Van Brocklin.

42. John McKay.

43. The Minnesota Vikings have won the Central Division more than all the other teams in the division combined.

44. Bud Grant.

45. 1979.

46. Mike Ditka.

47. 1982 was the strike year in which the Packers failed to play all the teams in their division. The players strike cut seven games from the schedule. The Packers missed out playing the Bears and Bucs completely, and only played the Vikings once.

48. In 1995, the Central Division

had four teams in the NFC Playoffs. They were the Vikings, Packers, Lions, and Bears. Minnesota won the division, while the other three tied for Wild Card spots with 9-7 records.

49. Trick question. The Central Division teams have represented the NFC in the Super Bowl five times. They also represented the NFL three times. Remember that the AFL and NFL were still separate leagues until the merger in 1970. While they were still divided, the Packers played in Super Bowls I & II, and the Vikings made it into Super Bowl IV.

50. Two. The Packers have won Super Bowl XXXI, and the Bears won Super Bowl XX. Trick question again. The Packers were in the NFL Central Division when they won the first two Super Bowls; they were not in the NFC Central because the NFC didn't exist yet.

5 - STADIUMS AND OTHER FACILITIES
1. Hagemeister Park was located next toe the Hagemeister Brewery.

2. When attendance for Packer games outgrew Hagemeister Park, the Packers moved to Bellevue Park, the home of the local professional baseball team.

3. The first City Stadium was built at East High School next to Joannes Park in 1925.

4. The original name for Lambeau Field was City Stadium.

5. Richard M. Nixon, then vice-president, came to Green Bay to dedicate the new stadium

6. 32,000.

7. 61,000.

8. Vince Lombardi was a better coach than a prophet.

9. 1976.

10. Gerald R. Ford, the President of the United States, when he was campaigning for the presidency in 1976.

11. The Packers played at State Fair Park in West Allis and at Marquette Stadium.

12. 56,000.

13. Curly Lambeau talked the executive committee into buying Rockwood Lodge as a training camp for the Packers.

14. $1,000,000.

15. The first skyboxes were added to Lambeau Field in 1985.

16. The Don Hutson Center was dedicated July 18, 1994.

6 - THE MEDIA
1. 1956.

2. WHBY in Green Bay, WTMJ in Milwaukee.

3. 1960.

4. Earl Gillespie.

5. Max McGee.

6. Ray Scott.

7. Tony Canadeo.

8. Jim Irwin.

9. George Calhoun.

10. Ray Nitschke.

11. Lee Remmel.

12. Art Daly.

13. Larry McCarren.

14. Paul Hornung.

15. Bill Jartz.

7 - WHO IS HE?
1. Forrest Gregg.

2. Emlen Tunnell.

3. Clarke Hinkle.

4. Don Hutson.

5. Lynn Dickey.

6. Buckets Goldenberg.

7. Curly Lambeau.

8. Johnny Blood.

9. Walter Kiesling.

10. Bart Starr.

11. Jim Ringo.

12. Willie Wood.

8 - NICKNAMES
1. Jug.

2. Johnny Blood.

3. Scooter.

4. Buckets.

5. Breezy.

6. Tiny.

7. Curly.

8. Cub.

9. Babe.

10. Fuzzy.

11. Boob.

12. Minister of Defense.

13. The Golden Boy.

14. The Rock.

9 - REAL NAMES
1. Bryan.

2. Joel.

3. Edmund.

4. Urshell.

5. Alvis.

6. August.

7. William.

8. Lisle.

9. Robert.

10. George.

11. Dwight.

12. Herbert.

10 - COLLEGE FOOTBALL
1. These guys were corn-fed in Nebraska.

2. Auburn, the other school in Alabama.

3. Yes, Marquette was once a proud football school.

4. Their nickname is Wolverines which is ironic since there are no wolverines in Michigan.

5. Our Lady of the Lake of the Woods, commonly known as Notre Dame du Lac du Bois.

6. Georgia, Georgia on my mind.

7. San Diego State, also known as Surfer U.

8. If you didn't say Alabama, then you didn't see Denzel Washington

and Gene Hackman in the movie *Crimson Tide*.

9. Bucky Badger would know that the answer is Wisconsin.

10. Utah State, established originally to teach BYU washouts how to be farmers.

11. Oh, give me a home where the Buffaloes roam: Colorado.

12. Did you know that Michigan State was once known as Moo-U because it was the agriculture college for the state of Michigan.

13. Sooey! Arkansas.

14. If you didn't say Minnesota, then you didn't see the 1995 movie *Fargo*.

15. Purdue, one of the best engineering schools in America.

16. Morris Brown, a first class institution.

17. Gonzaga, another college that once had a fine football program.

18. The Puritans wouldn't let the Irish into Boston U., thus was born Boston College.

19. Furman, another refugee of the antebellum South.

20. Illinois, a college that produces great players but never great teams.

21. Grambling, soon to be renamed

for the greatest coach in college football history, Eddie Robinson.

22. Beloit. Did you know that the William Hulbert, the man who founded the National League in baseball, was one of its early graduates?

23. Northwestern, the university that keeps the Big Ten's GPA up.

24. Oklahoma State, where slow Sooners used to go to college.

25. Yale, the place where smart kids go and once in a while a smart kid who can run and recite Einstein's theory of relativity at the same time, gets in.

26. Clemson, see answer 19.

27. Idaho, where future potato farmers go to college.

28. Arkansas-Pine Bluff, for kids who can't do hog calls.

29. Cal State-Fullerton, for kids who can't surf.

30. Penn State, for kids who can't get into Ivy League schools.

31. Southern Mississippi, started because Ole Miss began requiring its students to have the ability to read.

32. Arizona State, formerly the state teachers college, then they started playing sports.

33. South Carolina, which would have to change the school nickname from Gamecocks to Gamebirds if it was located in Massachusetts.

34. South Dakota State, always a small college football power, but what else is there to do in South Dakota.

35. Northeastern, an excellent school that couldn't get into the Ivy League.

36. Texas-El Paso, a basketball school that plays football only because it has to by state law or be ceded back to Mexico.

37. Florida State, whose nickname is Seminoles and rightfully so if you know how the Seminoles came about.

38. Kansas State, established so the soldiers at nearby Fort Riley would have girls to date.

39. Southern California, where rich kids go to party and attend classes where they learn how to look good while shopping on Rodeo Drive.

40. Southern Methodist, the reason Texas Christian University exists.

41. Mississippi, still fighting the Civil War and still losing.

42. Indiana wouldn't play football if Bobby Knight had his way.

43. Kansas, whose original nickname, the Sunflowers, was changed because opposing teams were always fertilizing them.

44. Maryland, nicknamed the

Terrapins because their early teams were not fleet afoot.

45. Oklahoma, where Texas oilmen send their handsome sons and ugly daughters to find wives and husbands, respectively.

11 - RECORDS

1. Tony Canadeo gained 1,052 yards in 1949, playing for one of the worst teams in packer history.

2. Jim Taylor gained 1,474 yards in 1962.

3. Jim Taylor gained 1,000 yards each year from 1960 thru 1964.

4. Terdell Middleton carried the ball 284 times in 1978 for the Packers.

5. Jim Taylor rushed for 19 TDs in 1962.

6. Andy Uram ran for 97 yards and a TD against the Chicago Cardinals in 1939.

7. Terdell Middleton lugged the ball 39 times against the Minnesota Vikings in 1978.

8. Jim Taylor gained 186 yards against the new York Giants in 1961.

9. Jim Taylor gained 8,207 yards during his career with the Packers.

10. Jim Taylor scored four TDs in a game three times: vs. Cleveland, 1961; vs. the Bears, 1962; and vs.

Philadelphia, 1962.

11. The Magic Man, Don Majkowski, threw 599 passes in 1989.

12. Brett Favre threw 61 passes in the overtime game against the San Francisco 49ers, Oct. 14, 1996.

13. Brett Favre broke Don Majkowski's record in 1994 when he completed 363 passes.

14. Brett Favre completed 36 passes in a futile effort to beat the Bears in 1993. Remember that game? The Bears intercepted Favre three times and returned two of them for TDs.

15. Lynn Dickey had two seasons worse than Favre. In 1983, he had 29 passes picked off, and in 1980, 25 were caught bay the opposition.

16. Tom O'Malley was a quarterback out of Cincinnati, and he played one season for the Packers. In his first game of 1950, the Lions picked off six of his passes as they blew away the hapless Packers, 45-7, in Gene Ronzani's debut as head coach of the Packers.

17. Brett Favre broke his own 1995 record of 33 touchdown passes with8 39 TD strikes in 1996.

18. Lynn Dickey knew how to get the ball down the field. He passed for 4,458 yards in 1983.

19. This mark is shared by Cecil

Isbell (1942 vs. Chicago Cardinals), Don Horn (1969 vs. St. Cardinals), Lynn Dickey (1981 vs. New Orleans and 1983 vs. Houston), and Brett Favre (1995 vs. Chicago Bears).

20. You looked! Your punishment is two free season tickets (section 17, row 14; that's about 50-yard line, about halfway up) to the Packers for all games including playoffs, but you have to sit backwards while your wife, girlfriend, or mother—who knows absolutely nothing about football—gives you the play-bay-play.

21. James Lofton could go long, catch the ball, and go longer. He caught 530 passes for the Packers, but he still holds the record for career yards with 9,656.

22. Don Hutson still holds the record for most passes caught in a game (14), most TD passes caught in a career (99), and most TD passes caught in a game (4), which he shares. He also holds the record for most TD passes caught in a quarter (4), which will probably never be broken bay anyone—Packer or whoever.

23. As time passes, most fans will forget Sharpe's attitude and recall his feats on the field. He holds the record for most passes caught in a career (595), most passes caught in a season (112), most consecutive games catching a pass in a game (103), most touchdown passes caught in a season (18), most passes caught as a rookie (55), and most touchdown passes caught in a game

(4) which he shares with Don Hutson.

24. Billy Howton was the greatest Packer receiver never to play on a winner. He gained 257 yards on seven receptions against the Los Angeles Rams in 1956.

25. If you weren't watching the Packers play the Bears on Monday Night Football, September 11, 1995, you missed Brett Favre hitting Robert Brooks in the flat and Brooks racing 99 yards for a TD that electrified the fans at Soldiers Field in Chicago and across the whole nation.

26. Robert Brooks had a great year in 1995 as the new go-to guy in the Packer passing scheme. He gained 1,497 yards to set a new one season mark for the Packers.

27. A serious neck injury ended the career of Tim Lewis, but not before he returned an interception 99 yards against the Los Angeles Rams in 1984.

28. Ted Hendricks only played one season for the Packers, but it was quite a year. He blocked seven kicks in 1974.

29. Irv Comp wasn't much of a passer, but he was a great secondary man. He picked off 10 passes in 1943 in only 10 games.

30. How bad would the '50s Packers have been without Bobby Dillon? In eight seasons with Green Bay, he hauled in 52 passes thrown bay opposing quarterbacks.

31. Willie Davis jumped on 21 enemy fumbles during his 10 years with the Packers.

32. Travis Williams ran back four kickoffs for TDs in 1967, and he had five for his career.

33. Paul Hornung scored 33 points against the Baltimore Colts in 1961 on four TDs, six PATs, and one field goal.

34. Chris Jacke booted five field goals against the Los Angeles Raiders in 1990.

35. Chris Jacke had 173 career field goals.

12 - UNIFORM NUMBERS
1. 26.
2. 31.
3. 26.
4. 24.
5. 86.
6. 84.
7. 89.
8. 74.
9. 13.
10. 64.
11. Don Hutson, Tony Canadeo, Bart Starr, Ray Nitschke.
12. 51.
13. 46.
14. 87.
15. 44.
16. 84.
17. 68.
18. 82.
19. 38.
20. 88.
21. 34.
22. 14, 3, 15, 66.
23. 31.
24. 91.
25. 75.
26. 88.

13 - WHAT POSITION DID THEY PLAY?
1. Center.
2. Defensive back.
3. Blocking back on offense and halfback on defense.
4. Punter.
5. Fullback.

6. Linebacker.

7. Tackle.

8. End.

9. Place-kicker.

10. Guard.

11. Quarterback.

12. Place-kicker.

13. Punter.

14. Center.

15. Quarterback.

16. Cornerback.

17. End.

18. Fullback.

19. Linebacker.

20. Guard.

14 - TRADES AND DRAFT CHOICES
1. MacArthur Lane.

2. Draft choices in the first three rounds in 1975 and rounds two and four in 1976.

3. Ron Hallstrom.

4. Detroit Lions, 1965.

5. San Diego Chargers.

6. John Hadl, Ken Ellis.

7. Babe Parilli.

8. Paul Hornung.

9. Ron Kramer.

10. 17.

11. Canadian Football League.

12. 1957, 1959.

13. Mike Butler, Ezra Johnson.

14. Ken Ruettgers.

15. Aundra Thompson.

16. Draft, trade (Denver), signed as a free agent.

17. Came out of retirement (free agent).

18. James Lofton and John Anderson; Eddie Lee Ivery.

19. Los Angeles Rams, Cleveland Browns, St. Louis Cardinals.

20. Cleveland Browns, Philadelphia Eagles.

21. New Orleans Saints.

22. 1936.

23. He could shuck and he could jive, but Terrell Buckley just couldn't play football in the NFL.

24. The Packers took Chmura in

the sixth round of the '93 Draft.

25. The Packers chose Brooks in the third round of the '93 Draft.

26. The Packers took Jacke in the sixth round of the '89 Draft.

27. The Packers took Timmerman in the seventh round of the '95 Draft.

15 - QUARTERBACKS
1. Rich Campbell.

2. Lamar McHan.

3. Cecil Isbell, Don Horn, Lynn Dickey (twice), and Brett Favre.

4. Tobin Rote.

5. Babe Parilli.

6. Bart Starr.

7. Cecil Isbell.

8. Randy Wright.

9. Jerry Tagge.

10. John Hadl.

11. Ty Detmer, although some might argue that in 1994 Mark Brunell was the first backup to Favre.

16 - PRO FOOTBALL HALL OF FAME
1. Canton, Ohio.

2. 1963.

3. Cal Hubbard, Don Hutson, Curly Lambeau, Johnny "Blood" McNally.

4. Clarke Hinkle, Mike Michalske, Arnie Herber, Vince Lombardi, Tony Canadeo, Jim Taylor, Forrest Gregg, Bart Starr, Ray Nitschke, Herb Adderly, Willie Davis, Jim Ringo, Paul Hornung, Willie Wood, Henry Jordan, Len Ford, Ted Hendricks, Walt Kiesling, Jan Stenerud, and Emlen Tunnell.

5. Curly Lambeau, Vince Lombardi, Bart Starr, and Forrest Gregg, although Starr and Gregg are in as players and not coaches.

6. Len Ford played less than one full season for the Packers.

17 - POTPOURRI
1. Alphonso Carreker.

2. Tackle.

3. Alabama.

4. Suspended (gambling).

5. Detroit Lions.

6. No college football.

7. Buford.

8. Lavvie Dilweg.

9. Michigan.

10. Quarterback.

11. Bobby Dillon, Willie Buchanan.

12. Francis.

13. Purdue.

14. Running back.

15. Bobby Dillon.

16. Boyd Dowler, Paul Hornung, Ray Nitschke.

17. Veryl Switzer.

18. Kenneth Davis, Robbie Bosco.

19. Jerry Kramer, Ray Nitschke, Paul Hornung, Jeff Everson, Wayne Mausser, Glenn Swain.

20. Skiing.

21. Steve Odom.

18 - HEAD COACHES
1. Gene Ronzani.

2. Marquette.

3. Scooter McLean, Phil Bengtson, Bart Starr, Forrest Gregg.

4. Phil Bengtson.

5. Broken leg when hit on sidelines by a careening player.

6. Curly Lambeau.

7. Scooter McLean.

8. Hugh Devore and Scooter McLean.

9. Johnny Blood.

10. Curly Lambeau (12-0-1).

11. 31.

12. Gene Ronzani, Lisle Blackbourn.

13. Missouri, Notre Dame.

14. Curly Lambeau, Vince Lombardi.

15. Chicago Bears.

16. Bart Starr.

17. December 24, 1974 and December 19, 1983.

18 Vince Lomdardi.

19 - VINCE LOMBARDI
1. Nine.

2. Fordham.

3. St. Cecilia High School, Englewood, N.J.

4. 89-29-4.

5. New York Giants.

6. 7-5.

7. Paul Hornung, Jim Taylor, Lamar McHan, Don McIlhenny.

8. 1962 (13-1).

9. Five.

10 Tied for third.

20 - PACKER PERSONNEL
1. Trainer.

2. Equipment manager.

3. Team doctor.

4. Scout.

5. Publicity director.

6. Public address announcer.

7. Trainer.

8. TV commentator.

9. Director of Packer band.

10. Radio announcer.

11. Secretary of the Corporation for more than 20 years.

12. Vice-president of Operations (General Manager).

13. First president of the corporation.

14. Co-owner with Curly Lambeau in 1922.

21 - STERLING SHARPE
1. 1988, #1.

2. South Carolina.

3. 112.

4. His own.

5. Billy Howton.

6. James Lofton.

7. Don Hutson, James Lofton, Carroll Dale, Billy Howton.

8. Don Hutson, Andy Uram, Johnny Blood, Bob Mann, Billy Howton, Max McGee, James Lofton.

9. Most Games, 100 or More Yards Catching Passes, 7.

10 Buffalo Bills.

11. Seven.

12. James Lofton.

22 - MIKE HOLMGREN
1. Curly Lambeau and Vince Lombardi.

2. San Francisco 49ers.

3. Steve Young.

4. Bill Walsh.

5. He is the tallest ever at 6'5".

6. Southern California.

7. St. Louis Cardinals.

8. Golf and tennis.

9. Ron Wolf.

10. Robbie Bosco.

11. Holmgren and Lombardi are the

only two head coaches in Packers history never to have a losing season, and they are the only two head coaches to take a Packers team to the Super Bowl.

12. George

23 - BRETT FAVRE
1. Kiln, Mississippi.

2. Lorenzo.

3. Gulfport, Mississippi.

4. Southern Mississippi.

5. East-West Shrine Game.

6. Atlanta Falcons took Favre in the second round as the 33rd pick overall in the 1991 Draft.

7. Two: Todd "I'm God's Gift to Football" Marinovich and Dan "WHO?" McGwire were taken ahead of him.

8. Packer boss Ron Wolf traded a first round draft choice to the Falcons for Favre in February 1992.

9. On September 11, 1995, Favre hit Robert Brooks with a short pass that Brooks turned into a 99-yard TD scamper against the Chicago Bears on Monday Night Football. No pass play or running play can measure longer than 99 yards because the field is only 100 yards long and the ball has to be inside the playing field which means no play can go the full 100 yards.

10. Four, as if you didn't know.

24 - REGGIE WHITE
1. White lettered in basketball three years and track one at Howard High School in his hometown.

2. Chattanooga, Tennessee.

3. University of Tennessee.

4. The Lombardi Award, which is rather ironic when you think about it.

5. The Memphis Showboats.

6. Reggie White was not drafted in the NFL College Draft because he had already signed with the Showboats and was already playing for them when the NFL conducted its College Draft.

7. 11.

8. 8.

9. 2, both with the Eagles.

10. Phil Simms, New York Giants.

11. Reggie led the NFL in sacks twice, 1986 and 1987.

12. David "Deacon" Jones.

13. Sara.

25 - GUEST TRIVIA
1. Hornung scored 176 points in 1960. This is one record that may never be broken until the NFL goes to an 18-game schedule.

2. The Packers didn't play on December 7, 1941. Their regular season ended the Sunday before. The Bears played the Chicago Cardinals that day and won to set up a playoff game with the Packers in Chicago the following week. The Bears won.

3. Green Bay was given the nickname of "Titletown" because the Packers have won more NFL titles than any other team in league history. They've won 11 so far.

4. The Packers had 38 players from Notre Dame before Aaron Taylor.

5. Thanksgiving Day, 1970.

6. The Browns won the first three meetings with the Packers.

7. Chicago Bears, 9-6.

8. New York Jets.

9. Chicago Bears, 33-6, October 31, 1994. Oh, whatta game!

10. The Packers suffered only a single defeat in 1962—to the Lions on Thanksgiving Day in Detroit. Lombardi was so mad that his team had been deprived of an undefeated season that he made the NFL change their future schedules to eliminate the Packers from having to play the Lions every Thanksgiving Day in Detroit.

11. Bill Musgrave.

12. Buck Buchanan of the Kansas City Chiefs. Fooled me, too.

13. Bill Curry.

14. All 60, 790 tickets were sold, but only 60,787 avid fans came to see the Packers in person January 12, 1997 when they defeated the Carolina Panthers, 30-13, for NFC Championship.

15. The Bears and the Vikings have beaten the Packers more than the Packers have beaten them. However, the Vikings lead is tenuous as they are only two games up on the Pack, 36-34 with one tie. A Green Bay sweep in 1997 would bring them even.

16. True.

17. Jim Taylor, 1962, and Bart Starr, 1966.

18. Actually, the Packers have had two quarterbacks whose ancestry included Native Americans. The first was Jack Jacobs, and the second was Joe Francis. Jacobs being a quarterback can be disputed because his official position was halfback, but in Curly Lambeau's offense, the halfback that Jacobs played was the team's passing position. In my estimation, that makes him a quarterback.

ABOUT THE AUTHOR

Wisconsin's best-selling author, Larry Names, is a prolific writer of both fiction and non-fiction books. He is a recognized authority on the history of the Green Bay Packers, the Chicago Cubs, and the Chicago White Sox.. He has written for newspapers, magazines, and television, and he has acted and directed for television and radio. He is an avid sports fan, historian, and memorabilia collector.

Names has authored 19 novels and eight sports books, including *Green Bay Packers Facts & Trivia*™, which, although now in its fifth edition, he counts only as one book. His historical series whose title character is Slate Creed has recently been picked up by Books In Motion, an audiotape book publisher. The first title, *The Slater Creed*, will be released on audiotape in 1998, simultaneously with the hardcover release of the book.

Larry Names was born in Mishawaka, Indiana, "plenty-one years ago" as he puts it. He is married to artist Peggy Eagan, and they have two children: Torrance and Tegan. They live on a 20-acre farm in central Wisconsin.

To reserve an autographed copy of any book by Larry Names, call the University Bookstore at 1-800-993-2665.

AUTOGRAPHS

AUTOGRAPHS

AUTOGRAPHS

AUTOGRAPHS